BOYS OF 66

The Unseen Story Behind England's World Cup Glory

JOHN ROWLINSON

TO JANE, MOUSE AND ANNA

1 3 5 7 9 10 8 6 4 2

Virgin Books, an imprint of Ebury Publishing,
20 Vauxhall Bridge Road,
London SW1V 2SA

Virgin Books is part of the Penguin Random House group of companies
whose addresses can be found at global.penguinrandomhouse.com

Penguin
Random House
UK

Text © John Rowlinson, 2016
Illustrations © Mirrorpix, MGN Limited, 2016

All photography supplied by Mirrorpix, except the following: p6, p57, p58, p59, p68, p217
John Rowlinson archive; p5 John Motson archive

John Rowlinson has asserted his right to be identified as the author of this
work in accordance with the Copyright, Designs and Patents Act 1988

First published in the United Kingdom by Virgin Books in 2016

www.penguin.co.uk

A CIP catalogue record for this book is available from the British Library

ISBN: 9780753557105

Printed and bound in Italy by L.E.G.O. SpA

Penguin Random House is committed to a sustainable future for our business, our readers and our
planet. This book is made from Forest Stewardship Council® certified paper.

CONTENTS

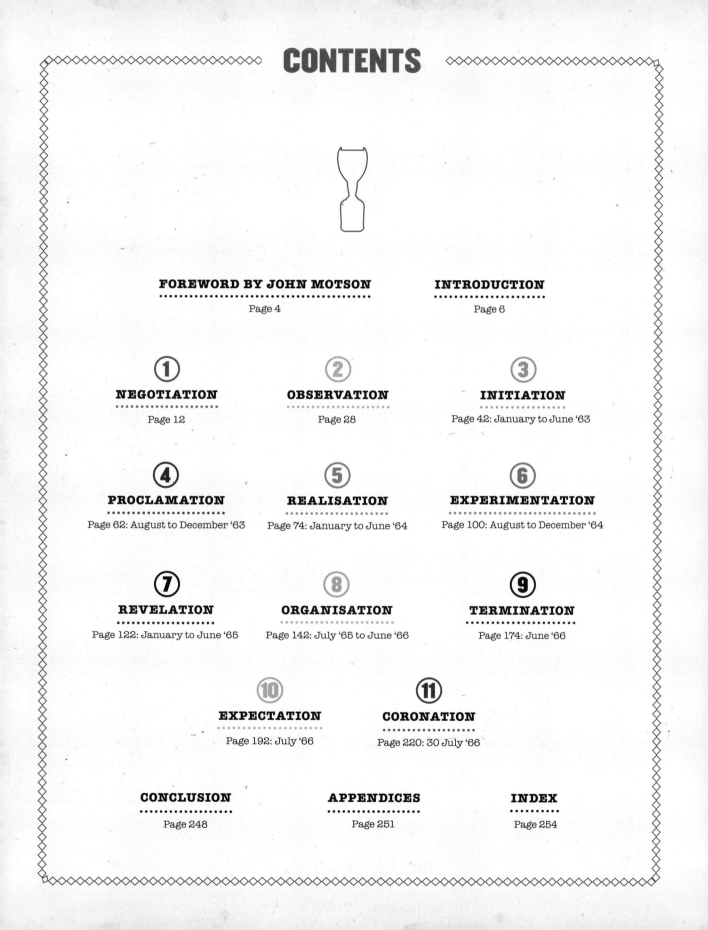

FOREWORD

Was it really fifty years ago? Those of us of an older generation will have no difficulty in recalling where we were and what we were doing that iconic summer when England, for the only time in their history, were crowned world champions.

I was a teenage news reporter, barely beyond the trainee stage, working in Hertfordshire, but curiously I was twice touched, almost accidentally, by the biggest football event to be held in the country that had spawned the game and spread it worldwide.

Part of my reporting beat was Finchley, so you can imagine how excited I was when the Mexican squad – including the famous goalkeeper Carbajal – announced they would be training at Summers Lane, the home of the Athenian League club whose games I was then covering.

It was a truncated connection. At their first meeting on Finchley's ground, the training session was shortened when they complained the playing surface was giving them sore feet! They never came back.

Alf Ramsey's England squad were staying at the Hendon Hall hotel, a few minutes' drive from Wembley and on the fringe of our circulation area. An invitation came to the office for a reception to be given by the Mayor at Hendon Town Hall. The England players, led by Bobby Moore, walked up the stairs of the grand building suitably suited and booted. Having grabbed the invitation from my news editor, I stood somewhat awestruck as the likes of Gordon Banks, Geoff Hurst and Jimmy Greaves picked a glass of something (champagne if Alf wasn't looking) off the trays held by the welcoming committee.

When the games started, a group of friends joined me for 'World Cup Evenings', when we gathered at each other's houses to watch the matches on our black-and-white television sets, listening to the voices of Kenneth Wolstenholme, Alan Weeks, Frank Bough and Walley Barnes.

My father managed to get a couple of tickets for the Wembley quarter-final between England and Argentina. I distinctly remember Argentina, with their neat South American passing game, looking the better side until Antonio Rattin was sent off.

I watched the final at a friend's house, in Potters Bar, before rushing off to a function in nearby Boreham Wood – a student exchange between English and German pupils, ironically – which I was covering for the paper.

But I digress. Ramsey's triumph did not start in 1966. I had been at school in Suffolk when he won the First Division championship with Ipswich Town four years

| John Motson with several players from his Sunday team Roving Reporters, 1966.

earlier, and much of that tactical thinking was a model for what he did with England.

Those formative years between 1962 and 1966 are the theme of John Rowlinson's book. He and I worked on a BBC TV documentary to celebrate the twentieth anniversary of England's famous win, and here he examines in detail the route that Ramsey took in selecting, examining and sometimes rejecting a host of players. Some got injured, some lost form and some were cast off mightily quickly.

A lot of them have their own story to tell in the pages that follow and we also learn what happened afterwards to those who did make the final cut. It is a book which skilfully captures the mood of the time and reveals that 1966 was a lot more complicated than a Geoff Hurst hat-trick and Nobby Stiles' toothless grin.

John Motson

INTRODUCTION

'The trouble with teaching history', a former schoolmaster once complained, 'is that everyone knows what happened in the end.' He said it was difficult to adequately convey the real fear of invasion of this country by Hitler's forces that was felt in 1940, when every schoolboy knew that the Battle of Britain was won, and that five years later the dictator lay dead in a Berlin bunker. So it is with sporting history. When results are widely known that leaves even less room for interpretation. Much has been written about England's 1966 World Cup victory over the years – for which this author in particular is grateful – but many of these accounts have hindsight shackled to the wheel, missing the bumps and twists in the road that accompanied the journey.

For some, the story is simple. First, England had home advantage. Second, manager Alf Ramsey invented a 4-3-3 formation, which proved effective, and shoehorned the players into it. Finally, stealing a script from *42nd Street*, when one of the stars dropped out a guy from the chorus line stole the show by scoring a hat-trick in the final.

Yet if the ending was so predictable, it seems strange that

'THOSE RAMSEY FINALLY DID PICK WERE MEN FROM HOUSEHOLDS WHERE THE SPOONS WERE RARELY SILVER'

with less than sixteen months to go before the start of the 1966 tournament, five of the eleven players who figured in the final were still to appear in an England shirt. The last piece of Ramsey's jigsaw, Martin Peters, didn't make his debut until May 1966: famously heralded by his manager as being ten years ahead of his time, he might well have been dubbed 'just in time'.

The truth is that in three and a half years, and 38 matches from February 1963, Ramsey chose no fewer than 50 players. Some, like Gordon Banks, were immediately effective; others, for whatever reason, found wanting and discarded.

This account, therefore, will be as much about assembly as arrival. It will attempt to explain how the England manager constructed a winning hand from the cards he was dealt. England's win in Madrid in December 1965 has often been identified as the turning point of the story, for example, but the team that evening might have been different had Jimmy Greaves been fit. As Ramsey once reminded Jack Charlton, the players he chose were not necessarily the finest players in each position, but the ones he knew he could rely on.

It helped that those Ramsey finally did pick were men from households where the spoons were rarely silver. Nearly all had been born before or during the Second World War and grew up in communities where money was scarce, rationing was still the norm and possession of a television set something that only happened to other people. This was an era when children created their own amusements. Greaves recalls football matches on bombed-out land, fifteen- or sixteen-a-side, which started after breakfast and finished at dusk. Any boy obliged to go home for meals would return rapidly to continue the game.

The lucky ones might catch the eye of a club scout and become an apprentice. But, as Norman Hunter recalls, that's when the work really began: 'There were quite a few of us on the ground staff at Leeds, and they'd have us on our hands and knees picking the weeds out of the pitch with a screwdriver. Then we'd be painting: the dressing room, the stands, anything which needed painting! Only when the groundsman had finished with us did we get to play football.'

Such an upbringing bred both spirit and strength of character, in turn reinforced by a stint of National Service during the 1950s. The two years of service, however, also created difficulties for budding footballers. It often coincided with a player's breakthrough as a professional, so that they risked losing their first team place almost as soon as they had attained it. Also, many actually lost money from serving their country. Until the wage cap was removed in 1961, all professionals could earn a maximum of £20 a week. During National Service, however, football clubs might reduce a player's wage to a mere £4 or £5 a week.

By the mid 1960s, the abolition of the wage cap had led to First Division footballers being paid well in excess of the average working man. But these were still far from the Premier League salaries of today: even Bobby Moore was earning less than £100 a week. Few could argue he and his colleagues hadn't justified their wages: the World Cup final in 1966 was Bobby Moore's seventy-third match of the season.

Compared to today's stars, players were much closer to those who paid to watch them. Ray Wilson recalls that, even as an England international, he would travel to home matches at Huddersfield Town alongside fans on the local bus, fielding alike messages of comfort and complaint. Loyalty to one club was also the norm: Wilson stayed at the Second Division club for most of his career, only leaving to join Everton at the age of twenty-nine. Of the eleven men who beat West Germany, only Wilson and Gordon Banks had played for more than one professional club.

The contrasts between players then and now doesn't stop there. Few of the boys of '66 had an agent, let alone a public relations manager. They owned a family car, not a Ferrari. Most liked a beer, but if they smoked, it was only tobacco. No one in Ramsey's team would have heard of, let alone chosen to inhale, nitrous oxide.

Yet in some ways they enjoyed more freedom than their highly paid successors. They played at a time when the media was less interested in football, and certainly less intrusive. Though *Match of the Day* had begun in 1964, live coverage of games was restricted to the FA Cup final, the England v Scotland international and a European club final. There were no sports channels, no celebrity websites and no magazines bidding for their wedding photographs.

Football stories rarely made the front page: in the case of the *Daily Mirror*, the biggest-selling paper at the time, it never made the back page either, which was also devoted to news until the early 1970s. The morning after the World Cup final, the *Sunday Times* gave England's 4–2 victory second billing on its front page, leading instead with a report of a lucrative order for Rolls-Royce engines. Nor was Monday's *Daily Mirror* any more interested in Bobby Moore and Co: its front page on 1 August was dominated by the news of a baby daughter for Princess Alexandra.

Though the final had been watched by millions, none of the English team were much richer for taking part. The twenty-two-man squad received £1,000 each, before tax, from the Football Association. Moreover, although some of the winning team received honours, with Ramsey himself getting a knighthood, it was only after a thirty-four-year wait that five of the eleven who played in the final were awarded the MBE. These days, as the mischievous Jimmy Greaves is fond of saying, FIFA gives a medal to the bloke who brings out the water!

The enormous salaries paid to today's Premier League stars means that when they finish playing, few will ever have to work again. The 1966 team never had that option: most tried, and failed, to become successful managers, with Jack Charlton being the notable exception. Twenty years after they scored the England goals in the final, Geoff Hurst and Martin Peters were selling motor insurance. Ray Wilson was an undertaker.

Yet all remained aware they achieved something on 30 July 1966 which may never be repeated, and did so staying close to their roots. The day after the final, Alan Ball stopped at a motorway café on the M6. He'd been the best player by a mile at Wembley, yet there was little fuss over his presence. One or two people asked to see his winner's medal, then left him to finish his egg and chips.

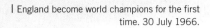

1: NEGOTIATION

November 1962. Manager Walter Winterbottom, in charge of England for the last time, chats to Jimmy Greaves and Bobby Tambling in the Wembley dressing room.

AS FAREWELLS GO, IT WAS FAR FROM SPECTACULAR.

The England team had done Walter Winterbottom proud, beating Wales 4–0 in his last match in charge in 1962, but as he left the pitch in the company of his assistant, Harold Shepherdson, there was only muted applause from the stands. It was perhaps not surprising: the crowd was a miserable 27,500, the lowest at the time for an England match at Wembley, an attendance not helped by a cold November Wednesday afternoon kick off. It also didn't help that the old stadium was undergoing a facelift, with cranes and steel girders dominating the skyline.

Once in the comfort of the dressing room, there was a moment to reflect on Winterbottom's 139 matches as England manager, going back to 1946. In that time some 131 players had been capped, many of whom had subscribed to the glassware which was presented to him by the England captain ,Jimmy Armfield. Alongside him were Alan Peacock, scorer of two goals, and Jimmy Greaves – in a Welsh shirt – who had scored the last and best goal of the match.

Peacock recalls that 'I had really been looking forward to my first ever match at Wembley, but there was no atmosphere at all. It felt like a practice match. I got a couple of goals, my first for England, but the second was a gift. Tony Millington scuffed his goal kick straight to me, and I couldn't miss ... It was a shame for Walter, who was a decent gentleman. More of a schoolmaster than a manager.

'I'd been with him that summer for the World Cup in Chile. Being picked to go was a big surprise because I was in the Second Division with Middlesbrough and hadn't been capped. But after England lost the first match, Walter chose me to play up front against

Argentina and we won 3–1.' Of the World Cup experience, Peacock remembers that 'We didn't stay in a hotel. We were based in a hill camp belonging to a mining company and split into groups of five staying in huts. It was pretty Spartan but I was with some good lads – John Connelly, Roger Hunt, Stan Anderson and Don Howe. I was the only one of us who got a game.'

England eventually went out at the quarter-final stage to Brazil. A few weeks later Winterbottom announced that he would be standing down as manager. Earlier in the year he had expected to become secretary of the Football Association he had served so loyally but had lost out in an election to the FA treasurer Denis Follows. Instead it was announced that Winterbottom would leave for a new post at the Central Council of Physical Recreation in January 1963. Until then he would continue to manage England and be part – but only part – of the FA's international committee that selected the team. According to his biographer, Walter Winterbottom later received a cheque for £5,000 from the FA for his sixteen years of service, with which he bought his first car – a Ford Zephyr – and also paid off the mortgage on his Stanmore home.

The committee's first job of the new season was to select a side to face France in the second edition of the European Nations Cup (England, like all the home nations, had not bothered to enter the original tournament four years earlier). For this first leg, the defence remained the same as that which had played all four World Cup matches in Chile. Right back Jimmy Armfield was named as captain following injuries sustained by Johnny Haynes in a car crash in August. As well as missing Haynes, a hernia operation had also sidelined Bobby Charlton, and there were four new caps alongside Jimmy Greaves up front. The match was played at Hillsborough on 3 October and turned out to be a triumph for the veteran French playmaker Raymond Kopa. Despite his prompting, England escaped with a 1–1 draw, their goal a dubious penalty converted by Ron Flowers.

The plan was for the new England manager to be installed by the time of the second leg in Paris the following February.

'[HE] RECEIVED A CHEQUE FOR £5,000 FROM THE FA FOR HIS SIXTEEN YEARS OF SERVICE'

RIGHT | Alf Ramsey with the FA's International Selection Committee. From May 1963 he would be solely responsible for picking the England team.

But two days before the first leg, the FA chairman Graham Doggart explained to his fellow members of the council that the search to replace Winterbottom had stalled. He revealed that there had been fifty-nine applications for the job as team manager, but that 'the committee were not satisfied that the man they required was among them'.

There had been an approach made to Jimmy Adamson, the captain of Burnley, who had worked as a coach in Chile alongside Winterbottom. However, the committee minutes added that 'the chairman of Burnley FC (Bob Lord) had indicated to Mr Doggart that Mr Adamson was not willing to be

considered as the England team manager'. As well as the justifiable speculation about Adamson, the press had also mentioned Dennis Wilshaw, the former Wolves, Stoke and England forward, as a possible candidate. There is no mention of an approach, however, in the meeting minutes.

Instead, it was agreed that Doggart should now 'contact the chairman of Ipswich Town with a view to approaching Mr A. E. Ramsey, their secretary/manager'. Doggart subsequently reported that he had spoken to Ramsey for two hours on 17 October and 'was most impressed by his attitude to the challenge which the post of England team manager presented'.

A week later, on 24 October, a lunch was attended by Doggart, Ramsey and Winterbottom after which, the minutes state, 'Mr Ramsey accepted the post, but asked that the announcement be made the following day so that he might inform the Ipswich chairman and directors before they read the news in the press'.

Unlike Walter Winterbottom, whose playing career was ended by injury after a handful of pre-war First and Second Division matches for Manchester United, the new England manager had enjoyed success at both club and international level.

Alf Ramsey was born in Dagenham in 1920, and as a young player had come to the notice of Portsmouth. They failed to follow up their interest, however, and after war was declared Ramsey found himself captaining his army team in Hampshire (he spent most of the war on home soil, rising to the rank of sergeant in an anti-aircraft unit). As a centre half, Ramsey impressed in a match his unit played against a Southampton side, and he ending up playing a few games for the south-coast club during the war. Following his 'demob' in June 1946, Ramsey was offered professional terms, turning his back on a career in store management with the Co-op.

As a player, Ramsey was still learning the game and had a stroke of luck when his manager, Bill Dodgin, suggested a move to right back. As the Football League returned to normality, he made his Second Division debut at home to Plymouth in October 1946. At that time Ramsey was second choice to Bill Ellerington, but when Ellerington was hospitalised with pneumonia at Christmas, Ramsey claimed a regular place. The following season he was ever present, and in December 1948 was selected for his first international, in a 6–0 win against Switzerland at Highbury.

A month later, however, Ramsey's fortunes were reversed. Suffering from a knee injury, Ramsey could only watch as Ellerington took his chance to reclaim his spot as Southampton's right back. Ellerington not only managed this, he went on to win two England caps of his own in the summer of 1949. By then Ramsey, unable to get back in the side and having fallen out with Dodgin, asked for a transfer.

In the close season, Southampton accepted a bid of £21,000

LEFT | November 1952. Alf Ramsey shakes hands with Prince Philip before the match against Wales. The game finished in a 5-2 win for England.

for Ramsey from Second Division rivals Tottenham, a deal which included the Welsh international winger Ernie Jones moving the other way. Ramsey was then twenty-nine, though some reports – which the player did little to correct – suggested he was only twenty-seven. The move was the making of Ramsey as a player. The new Spurs manager, Arthur Rowe, encouraged the quietly spoken, studious full back to express himself more off the field, and to expand his game on it.

The returns were instant. Ramsey became an integral part of the famous 'push and run' team, hiding his lack of pace in defence by shrewd positioning, while also pushing forward into the opponents' half – normally uncharted territory for 1940s' full backs. Ramsey helped Spurs win the Second Division title by a country mile, with his old team Southampton missing promotion on goal average. To cap his comeback, Ramsey also regained his England place in November 1949 against Italy – fittingly on his new home ground of White Hart Lane.

RIGHT | Alf Ramsey in action for Spurs, with whom he won Second and First Division championships in succession.

The following year, Ramsey was part of the England squad for the 1950 World Cup in Brazil. It was the first time England had played in the tournament: they'd chosen to remain outside FIFA's jurisdiction before the war and had not competed in the first three competitions of 1930, 1934 and 1938. Nevertheless, based on recent results and reputation, England were both seeded and considered strong favourites to progress from a group containing

Chile, the United States and Spain.

Preparations for the tournament, however, were far from ideal. A month before leaving, Neil Franklin, England's first-choice centre half, had accepted a huge financial offer to sign for a club in Colombia not affiliated to FIFA, which eliminated him from the finals. Stanley Matthews, meanwhile, had been touring North America with another FA party and was a late addition. As for Ramsey and the bulk of the squad, they endured a thirty-one-hour flight from London, arriving in Rio just five days before their opening match.

With so little time to acclimatise, England did well to beat Chile 2–0 in the newly constructed Maracanã Stadium. Next, the team flew to Belo Horizonte and then travelled by coach along a twisting road to their training camp. Ramsey, who had toured the country with Southampton two years earlier, later remembered the transfer well: 'Never will the England footballers who made the journey to the camp forget the nightmare experience of being driven around 167 hairpin bends on a road which seemed to cling to the side of the mountain.'

The England team's mood didn't improve when they arrived for their second match against the United States. The stadium and pitch were in poor condition and the players were forced to change at another ground, a few minutes' drive away. Even so, an English victory seemed a certainty. A couple of weeks earlier, the Americans had lost 1–0 in New York to the FA touring team. The Americans had since proved durable in their first World Cup match, leading Spain 1–0 until the eightieth minute, but had eventually succumbed, conceding three late goals.

On top of which, this was the England team of Billy Wright and Tom Finney, of Wilf Mannion and Stan Mortensen, with Ramsey playing his sixth consecutive international.

The match, however, was a disaster for England. The USA, captained by Eddie McIlvenny – recently granted a free transfer by Wrexham – took the lead with a deflected header just before half-time and somehow hung on for a 1–0 win. If an England team had beaten the USA at baseball there could have been no greater upset.

June 1950. The England squad prepares to leave for the World Cup in Brazil. Alf Ramsey is third from the left, with the England captain Billy Wright in front of the microphones.

'NEVER WILL THE ENGLAND FOOTBALLERS WHO MADE THE JOURNEY TO THE CAMP FORGET THE NIGHTMARE EXPERIENCE'

The scoreline made Belo Horizonte the benchmark for a shocking result in any match, a fact reinforced by the 7–1 thrashing handed out to Brazil by Germany in the same city in 2014. Certainly Ramsey never forgot what happened to England that day, nor that he might have been at fault with Spain's winning goal in their next match. It meant that England, just as in Brazil sixty-four years later, failed to progress from the group stage.

Back home, however, the post-mortem to the 1950 World Cup was relatively short-lived. Certainly the official *Football Association Yearbook* carried neither reports nor analysis of England's exit. Domestic league and cup instead remained paramount. Within a few weeks, Ramsey was back in action for Spurs at Blackpool. By now he was at the peak of his game, missing only two First Division matches that season and, in the absence of Wright, captaining England against Wales and Yugoslavia. In the league, Spurs held off Manchester United to win the title for the very first time. It meant Ramsey had won First and Second Division titles in successive seasons – a feat he would equal as manager of Ipswich Town.

In his personal life there was further happiness when he married Vickie at the register office in Southampton on 12 December 1951. Given that Ramsey and Spurs had a match against Middlesbrough three days later, the couple were only able to enjoy a brief honeymoon in Bournemouth.

Ramsey continued as a regular for both club and country. In November 1953 came the match that would define Ramsey's generation: Hungary came to Wembley and won at a canter 6–3, the first time England had lost at home to continental opposition. Perhaps the result had been coming: in a previous international against a FIFA select, only a late and nerveless penalty kick by Ramsey had secured a 4–4 draw. This time, against Ferenc Puskás and company, England were powerless. Hungary scored inside a minute and, with their swift passing and movement off the ball, were 4–1 up in half an hour. The match turned out to be Ramsey's final international; although he scored England's third from another penalty kick, it was clear he and his colleagues had been undone by a team who had worked endlessly together, and whose output was far greater than its individual parts.

In contrast to the corporate shrugging of the shoulders after Belo Horizonte, there now followed a strict examination, not to say an autopsy, of how football was governed in England. For all that their finances were buoyed by a combination of the post-war boom in attendances and that their employees – the players – being subject to a maximum wage, the Football League remained an insular assembly of clubs. Only two years after the defeat by Hungary, league officials – citing possible fixture congestion – persuaded the English champions Chelsea, not to enter the inaugural European Cup.

| November 1953. Alf Ramsey watches Gil Merrick gather the ball during England's 6–3 defeat at the hands of Hungary.

The Football Association, celebrating its ninetieth birthday in 1953, was an unwieldy body of councils and committees, with few full-time professional staff. In the case of the England team, the FA had always maintained that selection was the responsibility of the international committee: a grouping made up of club chairman and directors – all amateurs – with just the one professional, team manager Walter Winterbottom. At best such a policy led to inconsistency. At worst, it saw a chairman selecting a player from his own club in place of Winterbottom's preference, to the despair of the manager.

Writing in 1953, Alan Hoby of the *Sunday Express* summed up the need for change within England's national side: 'Sooner or later one man must be in charge of England's international eleven. He will supervise, select and coach the team … selecting and sifting (the team) is a full-time job and should not be left in the hands of builders, grocers, plumbers and traders, however successful they are in their own business.'

It would take another decade, and Ramsey's reappearance in the England set up, before that wish could be fulfilled.

GORDON BANKS

There are really two types of goalkeepers. The first can turn the good save into a spectacular one, like a high-wire artist who feints a slip only to conjure up an elaborate recovery. Gordon Banks was of the second persuasion; he could do spectacular if required, and produced in Mexico the save from Pelé universally regarded as near perfect. But Banks was also a man who made an art form of anticipation, so that his great saves looked merely good, and the good, commonplace. Modest and unassuming, he could leave even the finest of forwards shaking their heads in disbelief.

SUCH COMPETENCE was the product of talent allied to sheer hard work – from which, as his upbringing dictated, he never shied. His performances made the job of the headline writers easy: 'Safe as the Banks of England'. Mind you, given the state of the nation's finances in 1966, the England goalkeeper's track record was probably the better bet.

Like so many of his England colleagues, Banks' boyhood was a fair bit short of luxury. He was the youngest of four sons, raised in a terraced house in Sheffield with a steelworks at the end of the street. Money was always tight. For a time he wore clogs to school, on the front of which his father had fixed steel bars to give them a longer life. In the early 1950s, his father started a small betting business. One evening, Gordon's eldest brother, Jack, who had a disability, was walking home with the day's takings when he was beaten up by two men and later died in hospital.

Banks played in goal for his school, in the same team as David 'Bronco' Layne, and for Sheffield Schoolboys. But at the age of fifteen he started work as a bagger for a coal merchant and later became an apprentice bricklayer. It was work which, he always maintained, gave him the upper body strength required to be a top-class keeper. Still playing local amateur football, he was spotted by a scout from Third Division Chesterfield. To everyone's amazement, Banks and his team reached the 1956 FA Youth Cup final against Manchester United. Chesterfield lost narrowly over two legs to a side containing Wilf McGuinness and Bobby Charlton. National Service in Germany followed, where Banks met and later married a local girl.

In the summer of 1959, the young couple learned that Chesterfield had accepted £7,000 from First Division Leicester City for the young goalkeeper. Banks' wages increased to £15 a week. Soon he was in the first team which, in 1961, lost in the FA Cup final to Spurs. A year later he was named as a non-travelling reserve for England's World Cup squad in Chile. Ramsey first picked him against Scotland in 1963, and his faith was rewarded by a succession of assured performances over the next three years.

The respect between manager and goalkeeper was mutual, as Banks recalled: 'He was a wonderful manager. He was kind and honest with players, but he kept you on your mettle. I made a mistake once when, having played fifty-odd games for him, I left the dressing room saying, "See you next time, Alf." All he said was, "Will you?"'

'It was always a huge honour to play for England, but we should all have done better financially from winning,' said Banks later. 'The Germans made more money out of the final than we did. We were not organised at all commercially. We just went home. Imagine what would happen if an England team were in the final again!'

In fact Banks is probably best remembered for what happened in the next World Cup. In addition to his save from Pelé's header, there was also the mystery of why Banks was the only player to go down with stomach cramps before the 1970 quarter-final against West Germany. It meant Peter Bonetti replaced him – with disastrous consequences. No one can ever be sure if Banks was 'nobbled', but Ramsey was certain the absence of his first-choice keeper had been crucial. 'Of all the players to lose,' he told journalist Ken Jones afterwards, 'of all of them, it had to be him.'

By that time, Banks had been transferred to Stoke City to make way for a younger goalkeeper at Leicester, Peter Shilton. In the Potteries he was at the peak of his powers as Stoke won their first major honour, the Football League Cup, in 1972. The same season he was voted Footballer of the Year. That summer Banks helped to persuade Geoff

Hurst to join Stoke from West Ham, but the two heroes of 1966 were to enjoy only a short time together. In October, aged thirty-four, Banks was involved in a road accident. He wasn't wearing a seat belt and lost the sight of one eye as his head hit the screen. Life was never truly the same again.

Banks did play again for a while, earning good money as a one-eyed goalkeeper in the USA, but on his return to England in 1979 he found few clubs required his services as a coach or manager. A spell with non-league Telford United was brutally short.

'They asked me to help them, and I got them out of relegation trouble. The next season we were doing OK, but I had to go into hospital for a hip operation and when I came out the chairman said he was relieving me of my duties as manager.'

If, to this day, Banks feels disappointed that his knowledge of the game was never put to use by the FA, or a professional club, it's less out of anger than genuine surprise. Like so many of the 'Boys of '66', a roomful of international caps – seventy-three in all – proved no passport to success in business, or football management.

Of course, if he had a pound for every time he was asked about the save in Guadalajara, he would be a very rich man: 'Jairzinho gets down the right and I'm at the near post as he crosses. I'm scrambling back to the centre of the goal when Pelé heads it and is already shouting "goal". Because he heads it down, I can't just dive straight across – I've got to anticipate how high the bounce will take it. I'm diving backwards to get my hand to the ball. I don't know if I've got enough on it, but as I land in the side of the net, I see the ball coming down – outside the goal.

'The place is going mad. I'm picking myself off the floor and you can see me laughing because Bobby Moore, who's seen the whole thing, had just said, "You're getting old, Banksy. You used to hold on to them!"'

2: OBSERVATION

Even in training sessions there was an air of formality about Alf Ramsey, but the England players loved him.

ANY APPRAISAL OF ALF RAMSEY'S CHARACTER NEEDS TO DISTINGUISH HIS RELATIONSHIP WITH HIS PLAYERS FROM HIS DEALINGS WITH EVERYONE ELSE.

To a man, those that were in the eleven who won the World Cup, and even a few who weren't, have nothing but praise for him. Success can breed sentimentality when it comes to assessing the past, but there's no doubt that as a manager Ramsey engaged the loyalty of hard-bitten professionals – men who had been around long enough to spot the fakes, the foolish and the coaches whose instincts were to curry support in the boardroom rather than instill it within the dressing room.

Jimmy Armfield, Ramsey's first England captain, said, 'I liked him, and he confided in me to some extent, but you always knew who was boss. There was a bit of John Bull about him. He was proud to be English and believed there was nothing more important than representing your country.' George Cohen, meanwhile, recalls that 'I always found him a very warm man. He didn't care much for the press, but with us he was always first class. If he'd spotted something you'd done wrong in a match, he would tell you quietly.'

John Connelly, whom no one would accuse of compromise, is clear cut on the England manager: 'He was a brilliant and brave manager who knew exactly how to get the best out of his players. He believed you never got anything without working for it. People said he was aloof, and perhaps he was at times, but all of us respected him.'

Certainly, there was an air of formality about Ramsey. He would often call players by their full Christian names – 'Thank you for

Forced indoors by the weather, the England squad trains at RAF Stanmore. The new manager keeps a watchful eye on (L to R) Smith, Greaves, Charlton, Douglas, Tambling and Baker.

coming, Geoffrey' he would tell Geoff Hurst after a match. He was also probably the only man in professional football to refer to Nobby Stiles as Norbert.

At heart Ramsey was a family man. He travelled almost every day from his Ipswich home to his office in Lancaster Gate. He hated official functions, or indeed much of anything occurring in London's West End, and his only vice was a trip to the local cinema, particularly if a Western was showing. Armfield recalled that, even when the players were relaxing at the hotel during the World Cup finals, Ramsey would suddenly announce that John Wayne was on at the Odeon and they should all go: 'Alf would be out of the door in a flash, and we'd have to grab our coats and chase him down the street. You'd have the whole England squad running after him. He'd order twenty-six seats and then tell us to be quiet because the film was starting. He loved John Wayne.'

Away from football, Ramsey preferred to dress in a three-piece suit; meeting him you might take him for a headmaster, or perhaps the local magistrate. Only rarely did he let his hair down. Norman Hunter used to say that Ramsey sounded posh even when he swore, and Roger Hunt remembers the odd occasion when 'Alf would have a few whiskies, and then the "F" word would come out.'

For the most part the players shared his belief that, as a group, they were going in the right direction, even if it sometimes made uncomfortable travelling. Bobby Charlton was once persuaded by the other players to ask Ramsey if they could wear something cooler than the heavy grey suits issued by the FA. Ramsey promised to think about it, but shortly afterwards announced that he had thought about it and he'd decided the suits would remain. Furthermore, on official occasions, anyone who deliberately forgot the FA's metal lapel badge would not escape lightly: Ramsey carried spares in his own suit pocket.

Some believed his stiffness stemmed from a desire to disguise his upbringing in Dagenham. He always denied taking elocution lessons. Even if he did, said Jimmy Greaves, he should have asked for his money back! Greaves, 'from the same manor', delighted in occasionally embarrassing Ramsey by saying that a bookie from the local dog track wanted to be remembered to him. Ramsey would deny ever meeting the man.

Whatever the truth, when asked for a few words in public, or in radio or television interviews, Ramsey had a stilted, deliberate way of speaking, and a habit of inserting unnecessary words into simple sentences. For example, Ramsey was once asked if the players were putting in enough effort. He replied:'This I have never seen in the England team. Not in any match have I been able to say whereby this player has not put as much effort into his game as he is able to. A bad match is accepted as part of professional football, inasmuch as they cannot perform their best in every match they play.'

LEFT | Ipswich players and staff gather to present an electronic tea maker to Alf Ramsey as he leaves to manage England.

Ramsey was always suspicious of the media and the press in particular. He resented their intrusion into what he believed was his world and never understood why he should give of himself in public. Even after winning the World Cup, and almost alone of those who took part, he never wrote his autobiography. He never courted journalists, nor believed it his duty to do so. Ken Jones, of the *Daily Mirror*, said certain reporters felt Ramsey owed them: 'They wanted to be close to him, and tried be part of the team. Some of them were a pain in the backside. I got on well with him, but he was never a friend, and nor should he be.'

To illustrate the point, Jones recalled an encounter on the day after the World Cup final, when the entire world wanted to hear from the man who had masterminded England's victory: 'A couple of us met him in the car park on his way to a lunch, and asked him if he could spare a minute. "Certainly not," said Alf, "it's my day off."'

Jones also remembered a later occasion when his daughter was ill, but he had flown out to Madrid to report on the England team. When he got there Ramsey told him he should be at home, and that there were more important things than football. But for every example of decency – and there were many – Ramsey could often appear downright rude when pressed, or caught off guard. On the whole he disliked the Scots, and Scottish journalists even more. Once, arriving at Prestwick Airport, Ramsey was greeted by Jimmy Rodger, a particular pest.

'Welcome to Scotland,' said Rodger.

'You must be f*****g joking,' said Ramsey.

Such outbursts were not typical and considered harmless while the England manager was winning football matches. But in Mexico 1970 and the famine years that followed, Ramsey's disregard for priming relationships with the press and FA officials proved costly. The news of his eventual sacking as England's manager in 1974 was accompanied by the sound of chickens coming home to roost.

All that, however, was to come. Back in the mid 1950s, Ramsey was reaching the end of his playing career and was only too aware that if he wanted to stay in football he would have to shrug off his inhibitions, leave Spurs and seek employment elsewhere. It was

RIGHT | Alf Ramsey always resented having to discuss his tactics and selection with members of the press.

obvious by the spring of 1955 that a fresh breeze was blowing through White Hart Lane. The title side was breaking up, and manager Arthur Rowe was unwell. Ramsey had become club captain, but he was now thirty-five. When Danny Blanchflower arrived from Aston Villa, it was clear that he should be considering his options.

In August 1955, Ramsey accepted the job as manager of Ipswich Town, who had just been relegated back to the old Third Division South. For the new man, it seemed a good fit: it was not a big city club with equivalent expectations. Besides, the brewing family who owned the club, the Cobbolds, had a reputation for enjoying the good life and allowing their manager to operate without interference. Ramsey, it seemed, would have time and space in which to build.

In fact he achieved a near miracle. Ramsey won promotion to the Second Division in 1957, and then to the First in 1961. To the astonishment of all, and at their first attempt in the top flight, Ipswich Town then became champions of England. Since then only Brian Clough's Nottingham Forest in 1978 have managed to win the First Division title in the season after being promoted. And Forest's starting gun never sounded in the Third Division.

Ramsey's success was in building a team based on a sound defence, captained by centre half Andy Nelson. Leo McKinstry, in his wide-reaching biography of Ramsey, *Sir Alf*, sums up Nelson's thoughts on the man: 'He had this photographic memory. He knew everything about the assets and weaknesses of everyone you were playing against. I never once saw him lose his temper, which is unusual in football, but he could put his finger instantly on what had gone wrong.'

In attack Ramsey turned to Ted Phillips, who had been playing non-league football. He was not perhaps the most mobile of strikers but had a shot like a mule. When paired with Ray Crawford – a £5,000 Ramsey signing from Portsmouth – the results were instant. Their ammunition was in part supplied via an innovative tactic that Ramsey would employ later with England. The two Ipswich wingers,

'RAMSEY, IT SEEMED, WOULD HAVE TIME AND SPACE IN WHICH TO BUILD. IN FACT HE ACHIEVED A NEAR MIRACLE'

and in particular the spindly Jimmy Leadbetter on the left, were asked to relinquish the touchline and to launch attacks from a deeper position than normal. Leadbetter told McKinstry: 'It was a great system and it foxed so many teams. I loved passing, and felt that if I hit the ball past the full back and someone put it in the net I had done my job. Yet the full back was often quite happy because I had not actually beaten him.'

In that never-to-be-forgotten season of 1961–2, the collective brains of the other twenty-one First Division managers failed to solve Ramsey's counterattacking approach. Opponents such as Manchester United came off the field feeling they had dominated the match, yet somehow the scoreboard read that Ipswich had won 4–1. In April, Ipswich faced Aston Villa in their final league game. Ray Crawford, the only Ipswich player capped by England that season, scored both goals as Ramsey's team ran out winners. Ipswich's rivals for the title were Burnley, captained by Jimmy Adamson. But they could only draw at home and Ipswich were champions.

RIGHT | This Ipswich Town eleven played in almost every match as the title was won. Back row (L to R): Carberry, Nelson, Bailey, Baxter, Compton and Elsworthy. Front row: Stephenson, Moran, Crawford, Phillips and Leadbetter.

Later that year, when the candidates to lead England were being assessed, Adamson would again be obliged to give way to Ramsey. That, though, could wait: for the moment all at Portman Road, and the Cobbold family in particular, had some partying to do.

BOBBY MOORE

WHEN IT came to training, Jimmy Greaves used to enjoy sticking close to his pal Bobby Moore. For a start, he said, he was slow on the turn. He wasn't a great tackler. And not much good in the air either.

What Moore did have, as the mischievous Greaves knew only too well, was an uncanny ability to read the game: to know where the ball was going before anyone else and, having acquired it, to coolly make a telling pass. As a leader he was never one to shout and scream, but he had authority, and was coolness itself in a crisis. If he'd been a soldier, he would probably not have been first over the top, but the man who calmly worked out the enemy's strengths and rendered them null and void. Nobby Stiles, who knew a bit about defending, said of Moore that 'He was so polished that some people thought they could really rattle him if they got stuck in. But behind the elegance was an iron will and incredible judgement.'

Robert Frederick Chelsea Moore was born on 12 April 1941, the only child of Doris (Doss) and Bob, who doted on him. The recent biography of the England captain by Matt Dickinson tells of a boy who was almost obsessively tidy, whose shirts were never folded but had to be placed on hangers around the room.

HE WAS NOT AN OUTSTANDING SCHOOLBOY FOOTBALLER, BUT SHEER TENACITY TOOK HIM TO WEST HAM, WHERE HE FELL UNDER THE SPELL OF MALCOLM ALLISON.

As well as coaching him, Malcolm Allison taught Moore to live a little and to have absolute belief in himself. Diligent in all he did, the pupil made his first team debut in 1958, and, four years later, was a surprise pick for the World Cup party in Chile. He was given a chance in a friendly against Peru, the first of 108 caps, and when Bobby Robson was injured kept his place as England reached the quarter-final. On his return to England, Moore married his long-time girlfriend, Tina.

In 1963, Alf Ramsey chose him to captain England for the first time, and soon he had the job permanently. At first the two men seemed an easy fit. They were from a similar background. Both had worked hard to improve themselves. But increasingly Moore was anxious also to enjoy life outside football, and, with his blond good looks, the young man was much in demand, and as Greaves is quick to point out, he liked a good drink.

The West Ham manager Ron Greenwood recalled how, after an away match, on a Saturday evening, 'Moore would travel back to London with us in casual clothes, disappear into the toilet, and then emerge immaculately dressed to meet Tina and go out on the town.'

Not that Moore's social life seemed to inhibit his success on the field. As club captain he lifted the FA Cup in 1964 and the Cup Winners' Cup the following year. The World Cup win completed a unique hat-trick of Wembley finals.

In the build-up to England's victory, Moore had been tempted to leave West Ham and join Spurs. His decision to stay after 1966 was partly due to a hefty pay rise, and partly because he wanted to stay close to his business interests. Greenwood however was increasingly critical of Moore's attitude: 'It was impossible at times to get close to him. That detachment was a strength on the field, but didn't help in the small everyday world of a football club. I remembered him as a lad, full of enthusiasm and determination. It hurt that he could be so cold to someone who had helped him so much.'

Ironically that detachment probably served Moore best when he was accused of stealing a bracelet from a shop in Bogota just before the 1970 World Cup finals. The England captain had to be left behind under virtual house arrest while Ramsey and the rest of the squad moved on to Mexico. When he was finally allowed to rejoin his colleagues, he produced his greatest ever performance for England in the match against Brazil. There's an iconic photograph of Moore and Pelé embracing after the match, the picture of mutual respect. As for the bracelet, if it ever existed, charges of theft against Moore were later dropped.

At club level, matters came to a head at West Ham in 1971 when Moore, Greaves and others were found to have been drinking on the night before a heavy FA Cup defeat in Blackpool. There was talk of a transfer to Brian Clough's Derby, but Moore eventually moved to Fulham, where, in 1975, he enjoyed another FA Cup final appearance – against West Ham.

By then he had played his last match for England. Even for a man as celebrated as Moore, life became a struggle. For one thing, his businesses were in trouble, with one of them – a proposed country club – literally going up in flames. Football clubs didn't seem to want him either, and after short spells managing at Oxford and Southend he left the game for good. His marriage ended in divorce and later he married Stephanie, a British Airways air hostess he had first met after a charity match in South Africa.

But Moore had been diagnosed with bowel cancer, from which he died on 24 February 1993. His widow, in association with Cancer Research, has since raised more than £20 million for the Bobby Moore Fund.

Aged just fifty-one, Moore was the first of the World Cup winning eleven to pass away. He is a truly English hero: at Wembley, forever his playground, there is a statue of Moore outside the new stadium. Foot on the ball. Confident. Ready to take on the world.

3: INITIATION
JANUARY TO JUNE 1963

ABOVE | Alf Ramsey poses with the England squad ahead of their Nations Cup match against France in Paris.

WHEN RAMSEY ACCEPTED THE JOB OF ENGLAND MANAGER IN OCTOBER 1962, IT WAS AGREED THAT HIS APPOINTMENT WOULD NOT FORMALLY BEGIN UNTIL THE FOLLOWING MAY.

This would enable him to manage the handover to Jackie Milburn at Ipswich, while also taking charge of forthcoming international fixtures.

It also meant that, in the short term, the FA's international committee would still pick the England team, starting with the return leg against France in the Nations Cup in February.

The game arrived at an awkward time. The hard winter of 1962–3 had decimated the fixture list, meaning some players hadn't performed for weeks. The team selected showed just three changes from Winterbottom's last match, with Ron Henry gaining his first and only cap at left back. There was very nearly a fourth change: with Jimmy Armfield suffering from stomach pains, Don Howe was rushed to Paris as a replacement.

On the morning of the match, *The Times* had pronounced: 'This is an important moment for the new shepherd Mr Ramsey. Let us hope that his men do not play like sheep.'

But on a frozen pitch, England were soundly beaten 5–2 by a French team that had won only two of its previous seventeen matches.

All across the park there were problems. Up front, with Haynes still absent, the forward line of Connelly, Tambling, Smith, Greaves and Charlton lacked a recognised schemer. At centre half, Brian Labone seemed below par and would find himself out of the side for four years. But greater blame, according to the *Daily Mail*, was

due elsewhere. England crashed out of the Nations Cup, ran their report, 'because of a most incredible display of fumbling incompetence by goalkeeper Ron Springett.'

The last word on a sorry night went to Jimmy Armfield: 'I didn't know Alf before, but afterwards he asked me, "Do we always play like that?" When I said no, he told me it was the first bit of good news he'd had all evening. He didn't raise his voice, and on the plane back he told me about how he believed in getting the group right, and that it was not always the best players that made the best unit.'

England's next opponents, Scotland at Wembley, were an even stronger proposition than France. The Scots had been unlucky not to qualify for the 1962 World Cup finals, and, though they had ignored the Nations Cup, a team containing Mackay and Baxter, Henderson, St John and Law was always likely to be a handful. For the Tartan Army, there was also the small matter of avenging a 9–3 defeat by England on their previous visit.

England's line-up on 6 April showed a number of changes to the team that had been beaten in France: chief of them was in goal, where Leicester's Gordon Banks was now preferred to the long-serving Springett. There were debuts, too, for Gerry Byrne and Jimmy Melia, who had helped Liverpool enjoy a successful season

RIGHT | Ron Henry of Spurs was awarded his first cap against France but was never picked for England again.

back in the First Division. Maurice Norman returned at centre half and Bryan Douglas to the right wing.

Sadly, what might have been a true test ended as early as the sixth minute when Scotland's captain Eric Caldow broke a leg in a collision with England's centre forward, Bobby Smith. With no substitutes allowed, or even discussed, Smith eventually returned to hobble on the wing, but it was the Scots – a man short and with left winger Davie Wilson at left back – who adapted to the situation better.

A mistake by Armfield, without a winger to mark, led to Scotland going ahead after twenty-nine minutes. One match report described 'his tendency to caress the ball before he clears it'. The result was a swift Baxter tackle and an even swifter shot past Banks. Two minutes later, England were two down: nineteen-year-old Willie Henderson was tripped by Flowers, and Baxter sent Banks the wrong way from the penalty spot. As the Scots tired from being a

April 1963. The England team to face Scotland. Back row (L to R): Ramsey, Milne (reserve) Moore, Smith, Banks, Norman, Byrne, Flowers and Shepherdson (Asst Manager)
Front row: Douglas, Greaves, Armfield, Melia and Charlton.

man down, Douglas ran through the middle to make it 2–1 near the end, but no one, least of all Ramsey, could pretend that the ten men of Scotland had not deserved to win.

On the back of these two defeats, England next faced as tough a match as they could ask for: playing the world champions, Brazil, on 8 May as part of the FA's centenary celebrations. In its death throes – Ramsey's contract becoming fully operational on 1 May – the selection committee named a team with Ray Wilson at left back. The return of the Huddersfield man after injury was hardly a surprise: Gerry Byrne had been severely troubled by Henderson a month earlier and Wilson, despite playing his football in the Second Division, had been England's first choice since his own debut, also against Scotland, at Hampden in 1960.

Like Banks, Wilson would go on to remain first choice, but Gerry Byrne had not been forgotten: three years later, having not played a single international since the Scotland match, he was named in England's squad for the 1966 World Cup finals.

Apart from Wilson, there were two further changes to the team. Ron Flowers, who had first played for England in 1955, and had featured in every one of England's last forty matches, was stood down in favour of Tony Kay, recently signed by Everton for £55,000. However, the postponement of so many fixtures earlier in the year meant that the league season had still not finished and Everton, on the brink of claiming their first championship since 1939, successfully appealed for Kay's release from selection. The outcome instead was a first cap for Liverpool's Gordon Milne: 'I'd been a reserve for the Scotland match, but the first I heard about playing against Brazil was when Frank McGhee of the *Daily Mirror* rang our home. I was delighted because at that time there were so many good midfield players around. Take Tony Kay for instance. Tough as teak. A real fire in his belly. It was very sad what happened to him later.'

ABOVE | On his England debut, Gordon Banks is sent the wrong way by Jim Baxter who scores the second of his two goals in Scotland's 2–1 win.

Milne's career had started at Preston, where his father, Jimmy, had been a professional before the war: 'Our house was about 500 yards from Deepdale, and Dad was the club trainer – really he just ran on with a cold sponge.

'My parents wanted me to get a trade, so even after I made my debut, playing with the likes of Tommy Docherty and Tom Finney, I was training as a joiner. Of course the maximum wage was around at that time, but to make things worse, at twenty-one, I had to do National Service, during which the club only had to pay you about £5 a week.

'I had one stroke of luck. Our infantry unit had been trained to fight, and were about to leave for Kenya. But I got a bad throat infection, and was in bed for twelve days. By the time I came out the ship had sailed!

'I got back in the Preston team for good, and there was talk of me going to Arsenal and joining Tommy Doc. But by then Bill Shankly, an old pal of Dad's from their playing days, was the Liverpool manager, and, even though they were in the Second Division, with Shanks you didn't really have a choice! I was his first signing.'

In addition to Milne, there was another forced change when Jimmy Melia withdrew because of injury. He was replaced by Arsenal's George Eastham, who, like Milne, was the son of a former professional.

As well as being an outstanding player, Eastham's contribution to the game followed a legal battle from which all his fellow professionals would benefit. During the 1959–60 season he had asked his club Newcastle United for a transfer. The club refused, and even though Eastham's contract expired in June, under the existing 'retain and transfer' system, Newcastle still held the player's registration.

Unable to move to another league club, Eastham essentially went on strike, and for a while found work outside football. Finally Newcastle relented and he was sold for £47,500 to Arsenal in November 1960.

Following the abolition of the maximum wage in 1961, the Professional Footballers' Association and Eastham decided to test

ABOVE | Injury treatment in the 1960s could be primitive. Jimmy Melia bathes his ankle in cold water, but was forced to miss the Brazil match.

ABOVE | England's new engine room. Arsenal's George Eastham and Liverpool's Gordon Milne were given their debuts against Brazil.

the legality of retain and transfer. The Football League argued in court during the summer of 1963 that the system prevented the richer clubs signing all the best players, ensuring the league remained competitive. Mr Justice Wilberforce, however, ruled the method unlawful: though some aspects of the system were retained, Eastham and the players had won another victory against their employers.

That ruling, though, was still to come. Back at Wembley in May, Brazil, to the intense disappointment of 93,500 spectators, were missing the man noted in their programmes as E. Pelé. In fact Brazil were without not only the injured Edson Arantes do Nascimento, but also Garrincha, who had ended England's World Cup journey the previous summer.

The match almost began perfectly for England. With less than a minute gone, Milne had a chance to score with near enough his first kick of the game. However, it was Brazil who went ahead, from a free kick after eighteen minutes: a free kick which film showed was

ABOVE CENTRE AND RIGHT | The life and times of Blackburn's Bryan Douglas. One moment equalising for England at Wembley, the next tending his market stall in Morecambe.

taken at least thirty yards from goal. According to the *FA News* report, the outside left, Pepe, 'sent in a vicious swinging shot that evaded the tentative white screen and found the hitherto under-employed Banks going first one way and then the other, but never with a hope of finding the ball until it was too late'.

Ramsey's half-time language to Banks was rather more industrial, having earlier warned him of Pepe's ability to swerve the ball. England improved in the second half and managed to draw level six minutes from time when Douglas scrambled a goal from close range. As well as salvaging a draw, the pluses for the manager were the dovetailing of Milne and Eastham as the new engines in England's 4-2-4 formation. That and the fact that Bobby Moore was the outstanding player on the pitch.

So far Jimmy Greaves had failed to score for Ramsey's England, but a week later he was in superb form as Spurs became the first British Club to win a European trophy, the Cup Winners' Cup. Greaves scored twice in Rotterdam to help his side to a 5–1 win

ABOVE | May 1963. The Duke of Gloucester shakes hands with Gordon Milne before the Brazil match. The other England players are Armfield, Norman, Douglas, Wilson and Greaves.

against Atletico Madrid. A week later Wembley hosted its first European Cup final as Milan, conquerors of Ipswich earlier, beat Benfica 2–1.

On 24 May at Highbury, Ramsey had another chance to review his hand as manager when an England team faced a Football League side. His selection lacked Banks and Bobby Charlton, who were involved in the FA Cup final the following day, but interestingly the league side included twenty-one-year-old Geoff Hurst, converted from wing half earlier in the season by West Ham manager Ron Greenwood. The match finished 3–3 with Hurst scoring once, but he was not selected in Ramsey's squad for England's summer tour.

The first of England's three opponents, on 29 May, was Czechoslovakia. It was another tough fixture: their team contained eight of the eleven who had lost the World Cup final to Brazil a year earlier. Ramsey made two changes from the Brazil match. He gave a first cap to Terry Paine in place of Douglas on the right wing. Paine's club, Southampton, had finished only halfway up the Second Division, but his pace had contributed hugely to a successful FA

BELOW | Southampton's Terry Paine, who won his first cap in Czechoslovakia, being briefed by Alf Ramsey (left), and at home working as a furniture salesman (right).

Cup run, before losing narrowly in the semi-final to the eventual winners, Manchester United.

The other change was more significant: Ken Shellito, who had enjoyed an outstanding season as Chelsea returned to the First Division, replaced the injured Jimmy Armfield at right back. This meant that Ramsey was short of a captain for the match in Bratislava. Though Greaves and Charlton were the two senior players in terms of caps, Ramsey chose Bobby Moore to lead the side. He was rewarded by a first win for his England team.

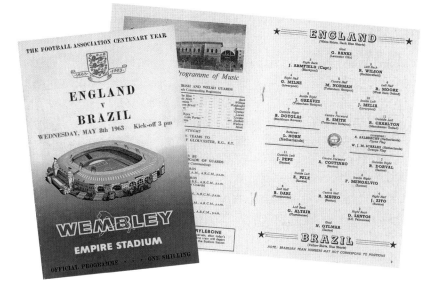

After early pressure, England broke away to score first through Greaves. He later recalled that 'We'd played in Bratislava earlier that season [in a Cup Winners' Cup match for Tottenham]. We lost out there to Slovan, when it was so cold even the Danube was frozen, but we murdered them at home. They had this good keeper, Schroif, but in the first minute at White Hart Lane Bobby Smith charged him into the back of the net. Almost through it! It was a foul obviously, and you couldn't do that these days, but he was frightened to death after that, and still shaking when he saw Smithy was playing for England!'

It was Smith who scored England's second, and a goal from Charlton and another from Greaves clinched a 4–2 win.

The performance had the *Daily Mirror*'s Frank McGhee positively

LEFT | The world's most famous football player, Edson Arantes do Nascimento, missed the England v Brazil match through injury, though was included in the programme (right) as E. Pelé.

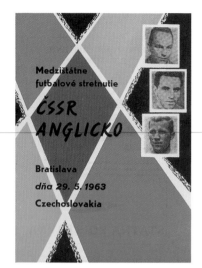

gushing with praise for 'an England side toying with a team which a year ago was rated number two in the world … Bobby Smith, keeping the Czech defence edgy and off form with the looming, lurking physical form of his bulk and bravery. Jimmy Greaves recapturing all his penalty-area piracy, and at the same time working harder than I've ever seen.'

Ramsey, less carried away, said simply, 'Today England played football criticised as old-fashioned, and it was both entertaining and successful.'

The next stop was Leipzig to face East Germany, a team who had recently knocked the Czechs out of the Nations Cup. Again there were two changes for England: Armfield returned as captain, and Greaves, who had gone down with tonsillitis, was replaced by Roger Hunt. The two free scoring forwards would become the focus of a rivalry that would extend right until the very eve of the World Cup final.

Hunt was a late starter as a professional, and said of his early days, 'I was twenty-one and had just got out of the army. I had a trial at Bury but nothing much seemed to be happening so I went back and played for my local team, Stockton Heath – Warrington Town they're now called. A Liverpool scout asked me to have a trial in a reserve match. I got a couple of buses to the ground and I'm sitting in the dressing room with all these pros, who were getting appearance money, and one of them was complaining about being dropped for an amateur.

'I scored a goal, but when we were 2–1 down the centre half told me he wanted to play up front, and pushed me back. I remember Joe Fagan, who was in charge of the second team, saying, "I want to see more from you." It was a bit of a nightmare. My dad came to pick me up, and he just said I should forget all about being a professional and come and work in his haulage business. But what Joe had said stuck with me, and so next time I started putting myself about and chasing everything. After five reserve matches I was in the first team, and in December [1959] Bill Shankly arrived and the whole world changed.'

In 1961–2 Hunt scored a scarcely credible forty-one league goals

'TODAY ENGLAND PLAYED FOOTBALL CRITICISED AS OLD-FASHIONED, AND IT WAS BOTH ENTERTAINING AND SUCCESSFUL'

in forty-one matches as Liverpool were promoted. He also scored on his debut for England against Austria in April, but was replaced for the next match by Greaves. Though Winterbottom named him in his World Cup squad, Hunt's more charismatic rival played every match in Chile. 'That seemed to be the pattern,' Hunt remembered. 'My England career was really stop-start, and I was always getting the blame if Jimmy wasn't playing.'

Now Hunt justified his selection by scoring the equaliser just before half-time, a tremendous shot from outside the box after Peter Ducke had put the East Germans ahead. Bobby Charlton made it 2–1 with twenty minutes left, giving England victory without playing well. After a goal in each match of the tour so far, Charlton then added a hat-trick as England romped to an 8–1 win against the Swiss in Basle.

Ramsey's changes in the Swiss match ensured that each member of the travelling party got a game, including a second cap for West Ham's Johnny Byrne. He, like Hunt, had made his debut for England under Walter Winterbottom. At that time Byrne was at Crystal Palace, in the Third Division, but then Ron Greenwood paid a club record fee of £65,000 to bring him to Upton Park in March 1962. At one stage there was talk of Geoff Hurst going to Palace as part of the deal, but that fell through and West Ham had reaped the benefit.

Against the Swiss, Byrne scored twice. There were goals, too, for the recalled Douglas and Melia, and for Tony Kay, finally making his debut for England. For BBC Radio's Brian Moore, later an outstanding commentator for ITV, it was 'A tour without a failure. Charlton and Paine were outstanding, and Moore showed himself as a future captain. Shellito and Kay – in just one match – assured themselves of a great future.'

Sadly, and for very different reasons, neither of them was to have a future of any sort with England.

BOBBY CHARLTON

SECONDS AFTER Bobby Charlton scored his first goal for England – a sweet volley against the Scots at Hampden Park – an astonishing thing happened. 'I was running back to the centre circle,' recalls Charlton, 'and there was a tap on my shoulder from the Scottish goalkeeper Tommy Younger, who congratulated me on the goal and said he was sure there'd be many more. Can you imagine that happening today?'

The sporting Younger was proved right. In all, Charlton managed forty-nine goals in one hundred and six matches for his country – a record which stood for forty-five years. That first goal came on his England debut in April 1958, scarcely two months after he

was found – relatively unhurt – on a Munich runway in the air crash which claimed the lives of so many of his Manchester United teammates. For a short time, understandably, he retreated to his family home in Ashington, driven there by his elder brother Jack.

But soon it was clear to the twenty-year-old, who had only recently held down a first team place, that he must return to help keep the club going. On doing so he found, in those terrible first few weeks, that his love of the game had not altered, and that he could best serve the memory of lost friends by trying to fulfil the enormous potential he had shown at United.

'They were the first club to approach me. I'd played for East Northumberland Boys and this little man Joe

me to come to United when I left school. Later I played at Wembley for England Schoolboys against Wales. There were 93,000 there. I scored a couple of goals, and suddenly a lot of clubs wanted me. I even had a trial at Manchester City and Don Revie asked me to sign, but by that time my mind was made up.

'But when I got to United I saw how many great players they had. Duncan Edwards was the best I ever played with. He had a presence; in any position he was just sensational. I had to really work hard to convince everyone that, from being one of the best schoolboys, I could make it as a professional. Those lads were a very good side and would have won the European Cup much earlier had it not been for Munich. And we were all friends, we lived in digs together. I still think about them to this day.'

Charlton's early international career did not always equal the excitement of his debut. Though he travelled to the World Cup finals in 1958, he was not picked for any of England's four matches. However, for small boys everywhere, he was fast becoming a national hero, based on the gentle nature of his personality and the less-than-gentle nature of his shooting. Older observers, too, came to worship, like Arthur Hopcraft in *The Football Man*: 'Something extraordinary is expected of him the moment he receives the ball. He can silence a crowd instantly, make it hold its breath in anticipation. A shot from Charlton, especially if hit from outside the penalty area, is one of the great events in sport.'

For a time Charlton served both club and country with distinction on the left wing, including England's journey to the quarter-finals of the World Cup in 1962. But his best position was in midfield, where he could better influence affairs, and still score memorable goals – not least against Mexico and Portugal in the 1966 finals.

Ramsey's team was always hard to beat, but Charlton was its inspiration, combining great skill and awareness with a boundless capacity for hard work. Jimmy Armfield said that 'I don't believe we would have won the World Cup without Bobby Charlton.' If further proof were needed, the West German manager Helmut Schoen paid Charlton the compliment of sacrificing his best player, Franz Beckenbauer, to mark him in the final. That season he was also voted Footballer of the Year as well as European Footballer of the Year. His only disappointment was United's failure to get beyond the semi-final of the European Cup. That piece of 'unfinished business' came two years later when Charlton scored twice in the final against Benfica.

In 1970, aged thirty-two, Charlton made his hundredth appearance for England, scoring against Northern Ireland. In June of that year, with England leading 2–1 against West Germany in the World Cup quarter final, he was substituted by Alf Ramsey to keep him fresh for the next match. The German comeback ended England's hopes, and Charlton's international career. His last league match for United was in 1973, and his total for the club he had joined as a fifteen-year-old was 759 first-team appearances and 249 goals. He then managed Preston North End, and played a further 45 matches for them, but when their board decided to sell a player without his knowledge, Charlton brought matters to a close.

Charlton went into the travel business, and was still in demand as a regular member of the BBC TV team on major football championships. At the 1978 World Cup, the BBC made a film of Charlton watching a coaching session, which gave him the idea of starting the successful Bobby Charlton Soccer Schools. One of the best 'graduates' was a young Essex boy called David Beckham. Charlton was invited to join the board of Manchester United in 1984, and was knighted for services to the game in 1994. His career, and his memories, now span more than six decades of changes in the game – from the England captain Billy Wright, on £20 a week, to Beckham and beyond.

Yet above all else, people press him to recall the events of 1966: 'Not a day goes by when I'm not asked about Ramsey and the others. Alf was a terrific manager, who didn't always choose the players the public appreciated, but men like Nobby and my brother Jack, he knew he could depend on. He told us from the beginning we would win the World Cup. That we had the players to do it. And when we did, at the final whistle, I just said to Jack, "Our lives will never be the same again."

'I have been very lucky. I love football and I love going to games. And I still can't walk past a ball without wanting to kick it.'

4: PROCLAMATION
AUGUST TO DECEMBER 1963

ABOVE | Alf Ramsey enjoyed taking part in England practice matches and would not
have taken kindly to the photographer who caught him falling on his backside.

THROUGHOUT HIS PROFESSIONAL LIFE, RAMSEY SHOWED RESTRAINT IN PUBLIC, PARTICULARLY IN HIS DEALINGS WITH JOURNALISTS.

A shy man, he was always uncomfortable with questions surrounding selection and tactics – questions he felt were none of their business.

These days the thoughts of the England manager are filtered through the prism of official, anodyne press conferences. In Ramsey's time, the press were camped outside the dressing-room door, and often travelled on the same plane as the team. It was a different era, and James Mossop of the *Sunday Express* remembered that 'Alf was always pretty distant with us. We used to call him Old Stoneface because he never felt it was his job to provide a good quote, let alone a story. You never saw him angry, or show much emotion – even after they won the World Cup! Everything was contained with Alf. Nowadays journalists have so much more space to fill, but the access to the team is worse. In those days you could wander into training, and it was easier to build relationships with the players, to have a quiet drink with them. I was based in the north and was close to Alan Ball and Jack Charlton; now you're lucky to get near the ground.'

It was a complete surprise therefore when Ramsey, in the summer of 1963, told a local journalist that England would win the World Cup. At an official press conference in August he was obliged to repeat the claim. 'England will win the World Cup in 1966. We have the ability, strength, character and perhaps above all players with the right temperament. Such thoughts must be put to the public,

'ENGLAND WILL WIN THE WORLD CUP. WE HAVE THE ABILITY, STRENGTH, CHARACTER AND PERHAPS ABOVE ALL PLAYERS WITH THE RIGHT TEMPERAMENT'

and particularly to the players, so that confidence can be built up.'

Ramsey claimed later he had made the original statement without first examining the consequences: 'something I don't normally do'. But he never retracted it – how could he? Some players, Roger Hunt for one, thought the prediction was a clever way of putting the pressure on Ramsey himself rather than the team.

On 12 October the first round of that season's Home Internationals was scheduled. England's preparations weren't ideal: due to an administrative error both England and Wales found themselves in the same hotel in Porthcawl. Ramsey was furious: 'It won't happen again. This is not the way I like to prepare a team.'

Welsh football supporters were probably more concerned to read that John Charles, recently transferred to Cardiff from Roma, would miss the game at Ninian Park. The match turned out to be a stroll for England, who were a goal up in five minutes: Bobby Smith scoring with a simple header past Hollins. In the second half Jimmy Greaves added a second and made a third for Smith, while Bobby Charlton, at the second attempt, made it 4–0 from close range. It was his thirty-first goal for England, passing the previous record held by Tom Finney and Nat Lofthouse.

'Ramsey to name World Cup 22' proclaimed the *Daily Mirror* the following Monday. Sure enough, he did, but the headline was a little misleading as it was merely part of preparations for the forthcoming match against the Rest of the World. There were two distinct teams in this latest squad.

The first was that which had beaten Wales, and would start unchanged for the match at Wembley on 23 October: Banks; Armfield, Wilson; Milne, Norman, Moore; Paine, Greaves, Smith, Eastham and Charlton.

The 'reserves' were: Waiters; Shellito, Thomson; Kay, Labone, Flowers; Wilson, Hunt, Baker, Harris and Thompson.

Of the nineteen who had toured in the summer, the chief casualty was Bryan Douglas. A veteran of two World Cups, he would not add to his thirty-six England caps. Jimmy Melia,

RIGHT | Bobby Smith puts England ahead against Wales in Cardiff. The Tottenham forward averaged a goal a game for his country and, as Alf Ramsey was to discover, proved a hard man to replace.

after just two appearances, also fell out of the reckoning and was sold by Liverpool to Wolves later in the season. By contrast, Johnny 'Budgie' Byrne and Ron Springett – on the sidelines for now – would remain part of Ramsey's plans.

The others in the squad were Arsenal's Joe Baker (holder of five England caps while with Hibernian), Tony Waiters of Blackpool, Bobby Thomson (the Wolves full back), Burnley's Gordon Harris as the understudy to Eastham, and winger Peter Thompson, recently signed by Liverpool from Preston.

The biggest surprise was the name of the other winger. David Wilson, like Thompson, had been a star of Preston's Youth Cup final team three years earlier. He had been in outstanding form at the start of the 1963/4 season, and would help the Second Division side reach the FA Cup final in May. However, of the twenty-two players named in this squad, Wilson was the only one never to play a full international for England.

The Rest of the World (FIFA) match was billed as the signature event in the FA's centenary celebrations. Ten years earlier, Ramsey himself had played, and scored, in the match in 1953 to mark the ninetieth anniversary.

This time round, the build-up was marked by a row over substitutions. Ramsey and the FA were clearly expecting a match according to international rules for friendlies, which allowed one substitute up to the forty-fourth minute, plus a goalkeeper at any time. However, FIFA had selected seventeen players for the match and were determined that all who travelled to London should at least be given half a game at Wembley.

The FA secretary Denis Follows met their stance with a shrug: 'If FIFA want to change their own rules it is up to them.' Ramsey, typically, was less relaxed: 'As the rules have been thrown out, I shall use eleven new players if necessary. There will be five reserves on the touchline, and the other six in the stands, but it won't take long to get them if I need them.' The Rest of the World programme notes included Pelé, whose club Santos were the world champions, but again he was forced to miss a Wembley

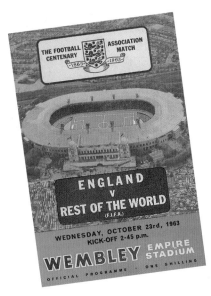

ABOVE | The England players applaud the Rest of the World team off the pitch after England's 2–1 win. October 1963.

occasion. However, the other sixteen players were used by FIFA in a match which turned out to be part contest and part carnival.

All the goals came in the second half, when the likes of Puskás came on for Eusebio – not too shoddy a substitute! Paine had put the home side ahead, but with eight minutes remaining Denis Law, who always regarded playing England as cut-throat, clipped a shot past Banks. Five minutes later, with just three minutes on the clock, England scored the winning goal: Charlton's drive was half blocked by Soskic, and Greaves – who else? – scored from the rebound.

There was one more international for England in 1963: again at Wembley, with Northern Ireland as the opponents. Ramsey made one change, giving Bobby Thomson a chance at left back. The Wolves defender was faced by Billy Bingham, both the captain and acting manager of the Irish team, but he found himself rarely tested. For the second time in four matches, England scored eight goals, and should have had more. Goalkeeper Harry Gregg, the Irish hero at Wembley six years earlier, was simply overwhelmed by their performance.

This time Paine scored a hat-trick, but even he was eclipsed by Greaves, who scored four. The other goal came from Bobby Smith in what turned out to be his last match for England. The Spurs centre forward had been a fine servant for two England managers and a scorer of fifteen goals in as many internationals as well as the preferred partner of and for Jimmy Greaves. But Smith would be

ABOVE | November 1963. Northern Ireland are thrashed 8–1 at Wembley with Jimmy Greaves (left) scoring four, Terry Paine (centre) three, and Bobby Smith (right) the other goal, in his final match for England.

thirty-three by the time of the 1966 World Cup. The search now began – throughout the kingdom – for the pair of feet which would perfectly fit his shoes.

As 1963 drew to a close, Ramsey could relax in the knowledge that a year which had begun in disarray had ended in such dazzling fashion. He had inherited a pair of full backs in Armfield and Wilson, who were now among the best in Europe. Moore had settled comfortably into a deeper role alongside Norman, while Charlton and Greaves, on whom so much depended, were conducting their own private competition to be England's top scorer.

To these Ramsey had added Banks, Paine and the midfield pair of Milne and Eastham. Performances both at home and away meant Ramsey's prediction of winning the World Cup was starting to look a distinct possibility.

RAY WILSON

IF EVER a good man were needed to stand tall in times of trouble, there would be a rush to select Ray Wilson.

Central casting, if he'd ever trespassed into the film business, would have made him a sergeant on the Dunkirk beaches. Straight-talking, with a wicked sense of humour, he would have kept heads up when so many were losing theirs.

James Mossop, who ghosted Wilson's autobiography in 1969, said of him:

'He was never happy talking about himself, but you couldn't find a fault with Ray. I remember the German manager Helmut Schoen saying all good teams needed a few players who could "battle", and Ray certainly did that for England. He must have been hell to play against.'

As a footballer with Huddersfield, Everton and England, Wilson was always clear-headed enough to know what he required from the game, and what he did not. After winning sixty-eight caps and terrifying a succession of wingers for a generation, Wilson was happy to settle back in the Yorkshire moors he loved and create a new life as an undertaker.

'Being in football for ever was not what I wanted out of life,' he explained. 'When I left Everton I had a few games for Oldham and then a spell as caretaker manager at Bradford but it just didn't have the right feeling for me. My father-in-law had an undertaking business, and earlier I'd worked there a bit in the summer to make up my wages at Huddersfield. When I stopped playing I told him I wanted to learn the business properly, and so I took all the necessary exams – hard work when you're about forty!'

Wilson's early life was anything but easy. He was born near Mansfield, the son of a miner, but his father was forced to give up the pits through injury, and his mother died when he was fifteen. As a teenager, he found himself living in digs and working in a railway wagon repair yard.

Though he had been a good schoolboy and youth player, it was only a chance meeting which took him to Huddersfield – 'it took me about five hours and three long bus rides to get there' – and an eventual conversion, while on the ground staff, from left wing to left back.

Wilson made his First Division debut in 1955, against the Busby Babes, in the season Manchester United won the championship and Huddersfield were relegated. No sooner had he made his mark than he was called up for National Service: 'After initial training, they gave us two choices of where we would like to be posted. I put England first, and England second. So they sent me to Egypt! When I got back hardly anyone remembered me. Before the maximum wage ended, clubs like Huddersfield had about forty or fifty pros on the books. There were some guys there who had had more seasons than games!'

In time Wilson became a regular with the Second Division side, and in 1960 was given his first cap against Scotland at Wembley. He and his wife took a bus to a pub outside Huddersfield to celebrate. Apart from injury, from then on Wilson remained England's first pick: 'It was funny. As soon as I got to that level I felt comfortable. The only problem was that some weeks I'd be playing against Brazil at Wembley and three days later turning out at Scunthorpe or Lincoln. I was happy at Huddersfield, but I'd seen my old mate Denis Law get away and do well. Eventually, in the summer of 1964, they accepted an offer of £40,000 from Everton, which was good money considering I was then twenty-nine.'

Ian Callaghan, who played against him in two divisions, as well as with him for England, always maintained Wilson was the best left back he ever faced: 'He was a quiet lad until he'd had a few beers. But on the field you never got a moment's peace. He was relentless.'

Soon after experiencing First Division football, Wilson was out for three months with a serious groin injury and missed all England's autumn internationals. However, Ramsey was happy to recall him against Scotland in April 1965, alongside two newcomers in Stiles and Jack Charlton. These three, together with Banks, Cohen and Moore would be virtually ever present until the World Cup was won.

In the final itself, the usually immaculate Wilson astonished his teammates by making a mistake that led to the first German goal: 'Every time I see that weak header of mine out to Haller on TV, I think why do I keep doing that?'

In 1966 Wilson also won an FA Cup winner's medal. But, two years later, he played his last match for England against the USSR – alongside his Everton teammate Tommy Wright, who was making his debut – and soon turned his back on football for good. He returned, without a single regret, to the places he loved: 'I've always been around the moors area – apart from those few years at Everton – and if you ask me what's my passion now, it's going for long walks. I don't miss football; in fact I honestly cannot remember the last time I went to a match.'

5: REALISATION
JANUARY TO JUNE 1964

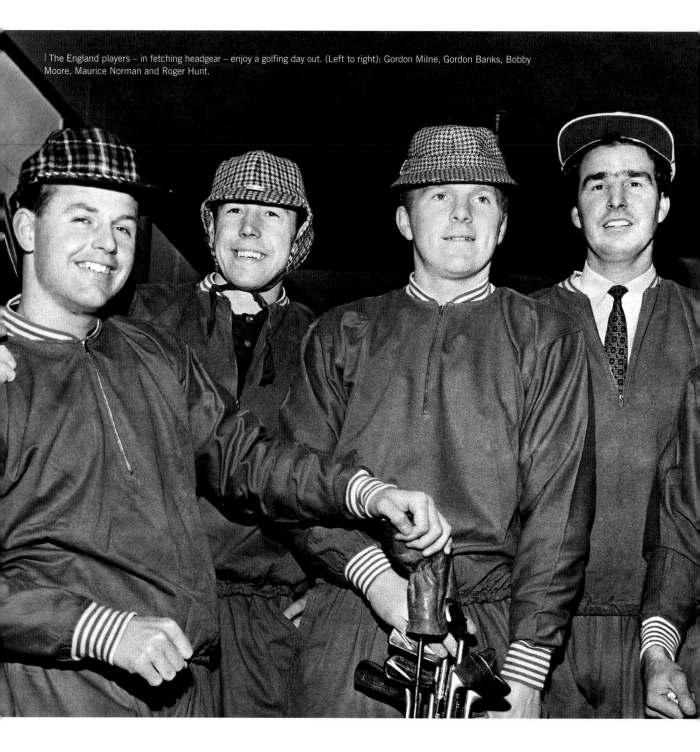

The England players – in fetching headgear – enjoy a golfing day out. (Left to right): Gordon Milne, Gordon Banks, Bobby Moore, Maurice Norman and Roger Hunt.

WITHOUT A FULL ENGLAND INTERNATIONAL UNTIL APRIL, ALF RAMSEY MUST HAVE WATCHED THE LAST FEW WEEKS OF THE 1964 FIRST DIVISION CHAMPIONSHIP WITH A TINGE OF REGRET.

His former club, Ipswich Town, champions two years earlier, were facing certain relegation. By the end of the season they had let in 121 goals, including a 10–1 thrashing by Fulham on Boxing Day.

The championship title had essentially been decided over Easter when Spurs twice played Liverpool. Here was another chance for Ramsey to compare the comparative strengths of Jimmy Greaves and Roger Hunt. Though Greaves would finish the season with the astonishing total of thirty-five league goals, compared with Hunt's thirty-one, both he and Spurs were – for this crucial moment – faltering. At the White Hart Lane 'audition' Hunt scored a hat-trick as Liverpool won 3–1. Two days later they repeated the score at Anfield, and would become champions for the first time since 1947.

Ramsey now had a tricky choice to make for the match on 11 April against Scotland at Hampden. He had Wilson fit again to play left back, and selected Johnny Byrne, in fine fettle for West Ham, up front. But, alongside him, Hunt rather than Greaves was preferred. According to the *Daily Mail*, 'Greaves will travel despite the loss of form which has cost him his place.'

Ramsey had twice enjoyed success at Hampden as a player, but it was not to be a happy return as a manager. England lost their third match in a row to the Scots; Alan Gilzean heading in the winning goal after seventy-two minutes. The newspapers were less than kind on England's performance, especially in attack:

'Byrne's flicks and glances had little effect,' said *The Times*, 'and Hunt now proved himself no more than an honest artisan as a spearhead.'

Ramsey himself made no apologies for a lacklustre performance: 'I accept the responsibility for not playing Greaves. It was not a gamble, the fact is that he has been blatantly off form.'

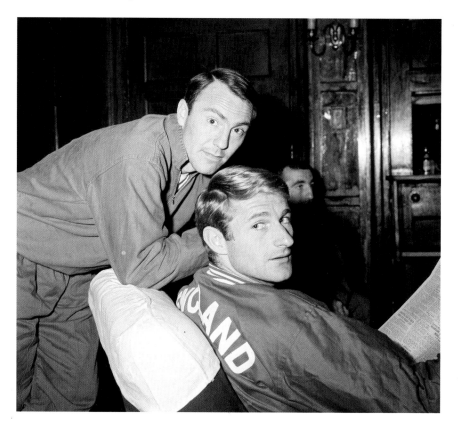

Whatever the Hampden verdicts, they were swiftly forgotten. The day after the match, under the headline 'Sports Scandal of the Century', *The People* revealed that three players – two of them England internationals – had conspired to 'fix' the result of a First Division match (see page 96).

The men named by the newspaper were David 'Bronco' Layne, Peter Swan (holder of nineteen caps for England at centre half) and Tony Kay, capped the previous year and still very much part of the England set-up. Though Kay had since moved to Everton, on 1 December 1962 all three players had played for Sheffield Wednesday in an away match at league champions Ipswich Town, still managed at that time by Alf Ramsey. They had each bet on Wednesday to lose, which they duly did: 2–0. Ironically, in their original report on the game, Kay was named man of the match by *The People*.

Swan and Layne were immediately suspended by Wednesday. For a while Kay denied the allegations and told the *Daily Mail*, 'It's a load of nonsense. In the match reports all the sportswriters said I was Wednesday's best player. Does that look as though I was trying to throw the game?'

For the time being, the absence of Kay from Ramsey's squad could be overcome. A much bigger loss was captain Jimmy Armfield, who suffered a serious knee injury in Blackpool's final league match of the season. Apart from the Czech match the summer before, Armfield had played in every one of England's previous thirty-eight games.

For the international against Uruguay on 6 May, Bobby Moore was the obvious choice to resume the captaincy. He had enjoyed a tremendous season, lifting the FA Cup with West Ham and being voted Footballer of the Year.

Ramsey's choice of a right back, however, required further thought. Armfield's previous deputy, Ken Shellito, had played only eighteen league matches for Chelsea following a knee injury. The injury turned out to be serious, and though he made a number of league appearances in the next two seasons, the man who might well have been England's right back in 1966 was eventually forced to retire as a player.

Ramsey instead turned to Fulham's George Cohen. 'Every professional wants to play for his country,' said Cohen later, 'but it took me a long time. I'd played eight times for the under-23s. Maybe that was a good thing, because I was twenty-six when I played against Uruguay, and probably at the peak of my physical powers.'

'I ACCEPT THE RESPONSIBILITY FOR NOT PLAYING GREAVES'

May 1964. Johnny Byrne (number nine) scores against Uruguay at Wembley.
For a time he seemed the answer for England, but his antics off the field did not
endear him to Alf Ramsey.

Over the next few months, Cohen would cement his place in the team, eventually eclipsing Ramsey's number of England caps at right back. Of his manager, Cohen was full of praise: 'Whatever his public image, he was very good with players. I had total confidence in him.'

The other more predictable change for the Uruguay match saw Greaves restored in place of Hunt. The headlines, however, were made by Johnny Byrne. He scored both goals in a 2–1 victory and gave notice that finally he might be the successor to Bobby Smith. Byrne's first-half goal had been against the run of play, but seven minutes into the second half a Charlton cross was helped on by Greaves, and Byrne scored again with a well-taken volley. Uruguay, destined to be England's first opponents in the 1966 finals, scored a consolation goal near the end, but it had been a dull watch for the 55,000 crowd.

For all the debate about Hunt and Greaves, it is not unreasonable to think that England's front two in 1966 might well have been the West Ham pair of Geoff Hurst and Johnny Byrne. The latter possessed skills which had managers purring. His West Ham manager Ron Greenwood called Byrne the Di Stefano of English football, and for a time the tribute seemed wholly appropriate. Byrne was not a big man, but with his back to goal, was blessed with a first touch and turn of speed that had defenders wishing they had tweaked a hamstring in the warm up.

Byrne was born in Surrey to Irish parents and became known as Budgie because of his constant chatter. He was a charmer, as Greenwood recalled: 'I once visited him in a hospital that was run by nuns. He had them running in circles for him – even putting his bets on.'

But like so many gifted players, the mayhem Byrne caused opponents was often matched by the way of life he embraced once the football was finished. 'I told him he should play for England past thirty,' Greenwood added, 'but he was not a moderate man and by the time he was twenty-eight his lifestyle was telling.'

For now, though, Byrne's stock was soaring. Having won the FA Cup four days before the Uruguay game, his two goals against the

'IF HE HAD HAD REPLACEMENTS AT HIS DISPOSAL, THE PLAYERS – AND THEIR PASSPORTS – WOULD HAVE STAYED IN LONDON'

South Americans at Wembley would, all things being equal, secure his place for England's next fixture in Portugal.

Before that match, there was a chance for other players to convince Alf Ramsey of their case for selection. On 9 May a Football League side faced an Italian League team in Milan, with the English eleven including a number of players on the fringe of the full team. These included Tony Waiters in goal, Peter Thompson on the wing and two players who had recently changed clubs for expensive fees – Alan Mullery of Spurs and Fred Pickering of Everton.

With Paine on one wing and Thompson on the other, Bobby Charlton was given a midfield role from the start, in partnership with Mullery. While the game ended in a win for the Italians, the real bonus, according to the *Daily Mail*, was the form of Thompson, who now seemed certain to earn his first full cap against the Portuguese in Lisbon.

The Portugal match was the first of six England away matches in twenty days: the end-of-season tour included three games in Brazil as part of the 'Little World Cup' – a four-team tournament to celebrate the fiftieth anniversary of the Brazilian FA.

But before the tour took place, there was an incident involving senior members of the team that, with hindsight, is central to understanding the precise relationship between Ramsey and his players.

The England squad had been booked on a Thursday morning flight to Lisbon. The previous evening, Ramsey told them that if they wanted to leave the hotel for any reason they must be back by 10.30 p.m.

In the players' minds, there was only one reason for going out – to have a quiet drink out of sight of the management. Not for the first time, the initial idea, and indeed the itinerary, was the work of Jimmy Greaves, ably assisted by the captain Bobby Moore and the party boy Johnny Byrne. The other escapees were Banks, Wilson, Eastham and Charlton.

The players ended up at a favourite West End haunt of Greaves, The Beachcomber. By the time it was decided to head back, the curfew had passed. Given the years that have elapsed, it is

understandable if all memories do not match: Charlton believes it
was not yet midnight; Banks says it was around 1 a.m.

Whatever the time, Ramsey and his assistant Harold Shepherdson
had already made a round of hotel rooms at 10.30 p.m. and placed
the player's passport on the bed of each absentee.

The inference was clear, though Ramsey waited until the end of
the first training session in Lisbon before summoning the
miscreants. Ramsey made clear that if he had had replacements at
his disposal, the players – and their passports – would have stayed
in London.

His next move, however, was to pick all seven for the match
against Portugal. He was rewarded by a magnificent performance,

not least by Byrne, who scored a hat-trick in a 4–3 win. His last goal, three minutes from time, was a piece of impudence, as described by the *Daily Mail*: 'Three defenders faced him. He beat two by doing nothing, then chipped the ball over a wall of shirts for a goal that was sheer robbery.' Peter Thompson, on his debut, made England's other goal for Charlton, while the Portuguese scorers were Eusebio and Torres, who would trouble England again.

Byrne's scoring run continued in England's next match against the Republic of Ireland in Dublin. He scored his sixth goal in three matches as England won 3–1, a goal that rubbed salt into the wounds of the home side: the Irish captain, Noel Cantwell, was not alone in feeling that, given his parentage, Byrne should perhaps

have been playing for the other team. England's other scorers were Eastham – his first for his country – and Greaves. The game also marked a return for Flowers, replacing Norman, and a debut in goal for Tony Waiters.

The Blackpool keeper was another player who made a late entry to the professional game, though it was not for want of trying. 'While on National Service,' Waiters recalled, 'I played a few reserve games for Middlesbrough. Cloughie was in the first team and his mate Peter Taylor in goal.' Nothing came of it – a situation that was repeated when he was recommended to Blackburn while working as a lifeguard near his Southport home. After two more clubs had rejected him, Waiters, now twenty-one, was still an amateur, combining his studies with outings in Blackpool reserves.

He made his first team debut on Boxing Day 1959 – 'though they still called me the amateur' – and occasionally pinched himself to be

playing in the same team as Stanley Matthews. When his rival Gordon West was sold to Everton in March 1962, Waiters felt he had finally made it as a professional.

For England, however, he was still the number two, and for the next match against the USA, Gordon Banks was recalled into the side. Quite why the schedule required the team to stop over in New York, only the FA could fathom. Some surmised that England's 10–0 win in front of just 5,000 fans was Alf Ramsey's way of getting the result in Belo Horizonte fourteen years earlier out of his system.

Only three players could look back with fondness on the match, two of whom were making their debuts. The first was Mike Bailey of Charlton Athletic; he had joined the tour late in place of Mullery, who had collapsed with a back injury while shaving. The second was Fred Pickering, who scored a hat-trick against the Americans. Even

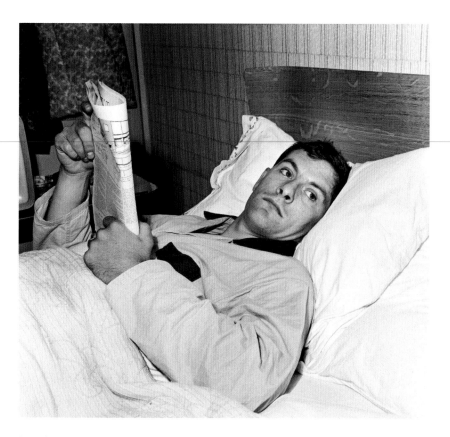

he, though, was outgunned by the four goals that were scored by Roger Hunt.

The next game against world champions Brazil was always going to be a sterner test – not helped by it being played barely thirty-six hours after England landed in Rio from a nine-and-half-hour flight. In goal, Ramsey switched his keepers again, with Waiters preferred to Banks. 'I honestly felt I could compete with Banksy at that time,' recalled Waiters. 'I also thought we played really well in the Maracanã but ran out of steam. We'd had a crazy few days getting on and off planes, and some of the team were struggling in the heat.'

The temperature was something that Gordon Milne also remembered: 'It was very hot. And because they had a moat round the ground, they also had ball boys putting the ball down as soon as it went out of play. You never got a breather.'

In fact, the Brazilians, who led 1–0 at half-time, had kept England waiting in the dressing room for almost an hour before the match in

'IF SOME OF THE PLAYERS WERE "NOT THE SOLUTIONS THEY PROMISED TO BE, THE ANSWER WAS HERE ALL THE TIME." HIS NAME WAS BOBBY CHARLTON'

a sly piece of gamesmanship. The humid conditions were certainly troubling George Cohen, and the England doctor advised him to come off at half-time. Somehow he and England kept going, and soon after the break Greaves equalised after Eastham hit the bar.

But then Pelé showed his class, scoring one and making two more goals in a nine-minute spell that changed the game. Waiters could not be faulted, though he was angry about Brazil's final goal, which made the score 5–1: 'Alf had decided we should have a six-man wall for their free kicks because they could bend the ball. All it meant was that I couldn't see properly.'

The scoreline flattered the hosts, and Bobby Moore said afterwards, 'We were not this bad. The difference was one man, Pelé. Me and Maurice (Norman) hit him with more tackles than we dared hope, but he still kept coming through.'

With a short break before the next game in São Paolo against Portugal, the players enjoyed a taste of beach life from their hotel overlooking Sugarloaf Mountain. Even on the Copacabana, however, the Atlantic current can cause surprises.

At one stage Budgie Byrne found himself helpless among the big rollers, his appeals ignored by colleagues, who reckoned it was merely one of his old tricks. Fortunately – and the former lifeguard Tony Waiters swears he was not the rescuer – he was pulled out before the old joke about 'not waving but drowning' became reality.

Ramsey, unsurprisingly, was not amused by such antics. Nor was he a day or so later when, at a reception given by the British Embassy, Byrne pushed Greaves – in his official England suit – into the swimming pool.

Despite these antics, Byrne kept his place for the match against Portugal, as Ramsey gambled on attacking power. He chose to pair Hunt and Greaves alongside him, with Paine and Peter Thompson – the outstanding player on the tour – on the wings. In all there were six changes from the Brazil game, including Bobby Thomson coming in at right back for the ailing Cohen.

The attacking gamble was not a success, though the Portuguese goal by Peres was a lucky deflection off Flowers. Hunt scored a

OVERLEAF | Peter Thompson, surrounded by his Liverpool teammates, poses with his fiancée as he opens his new garage close to Anfield. The unlucky Thompson was left out of Ramsey's final World Cup squads in both 1966 and 1970.

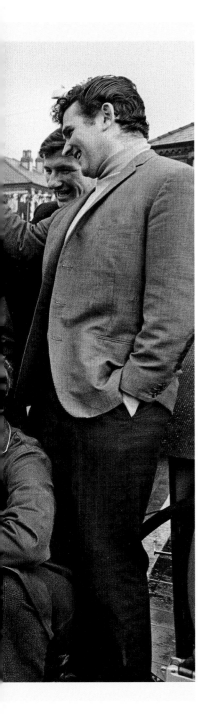

superb equaliser, and both he and Byrne had goals disallowed. When a Coluna effort was ruled out, the Portuguese players hounded the referee and officials for a full five minutes, ending only when Torres was sent off.

The eleventh and final international of a long season was played back in Rio against Argentina, who had earlier beaten Brazil 3–0 in a match marred by violence on and off the field. Ramsey and his squad had watched from the stands but been forced to leave when some members of the Brazilian crowd – no doubt irritated by Ray Wilson sticking up three fingers to underline the score – started to throw fruit at them. 'That's right, Ray, you appease them,' said Greaves as the soggy bullets flew.

Against England on 6 June, Antonio Rattin marshalled a defensive line-up to which Ramsey's men had no answer, though Thompson again tormented both full backs. Brian James in the *Daily Mail* was clear that 'Argentina allowed England to batter them for most of the game, watching all the while for one chance.' When it arrived, Chaldu playing in Rojas to score past Banks in the seventy-fourth minute, both forwards looked suspiciously offside.

With a first complete season as England manager behind him, Ramsey had four months before the next match to reflect on both players and formations. Provided they did not run into Pelé on a weekly basis, England's defence seemed solid, even if Cohen had still to prove himself the true successor to Armfield.

The problems instead were further forward. Though Ramsey's preference remained for 4-2-4, there was a risk that, with two wingers hugging the touchlines, Milne and Eastham could be overrun in midfield. And Ramsey, to his very fingertips, was risk-averse.

The other question was, when faced with the likes of Argentina, did England possess a world-class player with the ability to transform a game? It turned out – as in the famous song from *Evita* – that if some of the players were 'not the solutions they promised to be, the answer was here all the time.' His name was Bobby Charlton.

GEORGE COHEN

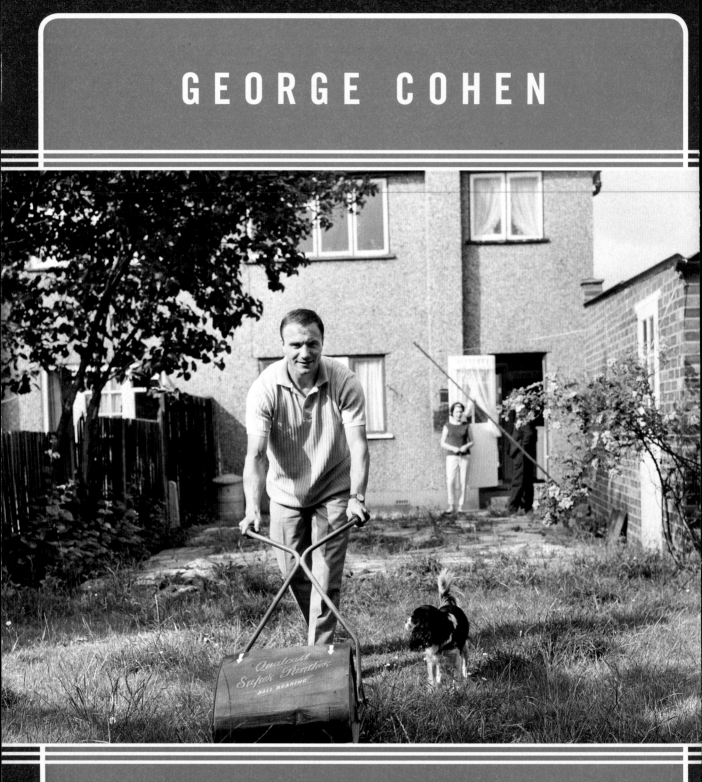

GEORGE COHEN was the first of the 'Boys of '66' to finish playing football. In December 1967, he damaged a knee cartilage in a tackle with Liverpool's Peter Thompson. While recovering, he damaged the other one. It was soon clear that, at the age of just twenty-nine, he would have to find a new career.

A friend of Jimmy Greaves in the building business offered him a job as a land buyer, but the adjustment was not easy: 'I had to learn a new profession from scratch. As a footballer everything was done for you. From the age of sixteen I never had to fend for myself.' Cohen now brought the dogged determination to business that he had shown in winning thirty-seven England caps while playing for an unfashionable club like Fulham. He eventually started his own property company.

In 1974 Cohen became ill, and was told he had cancer: 'I needed an immediate operation. The children were young, and were not aware of anything wrong until they were older. I had six months of hospital and treatment, but a year later it came back. It was an awful time, because I was still trying to run a company. I got better, but at Christmas 1980 the cancer came back and it looked bad. But I was looked after by a marvellous specialist at the Royal Marsden and, thanks largely to my wife, Daphne, we got through it in the end.'

Cohen was successful in business and now lives in Kent – a more rural environment than the one he knew as a child. Born the month after war broke out in 1939, he was brought up in West Kensington. Cohen recalled: 'That was the part of Fulham, we used to say, where the children had shoes.' At one stage he had thoughts of being a boxer, but joined Fulham, and played alongside Johnny Haynes, Jimmy Hill and Alan Mullery in the side that won promotion to the First Division in 1959.

It took time for Cohen to establish himself, but when Jimmy Armfield was injured in April 1964, Cohen was picked at the age of twenty-six to play his first match for England, and would remain Ramsey's first choice: 'I liked Alf. He only ever asked you to do what you were capable of. I liked to get forward, and the lads used to tease me about my crosses being more dangerous to the crowd than our opponents, but primarily I thought I was a good defender in a back four where we all knew our jobs.

'Looking back, there were two remarkable things about that team. First, that we all got on so well, except Jack of course, who was always arguing about something! Second, that we had total confidence in the manager. He was a kind and sensitive man, though he never came over like that in public, and his wife is charming. But even Alf could lose it sometimes. I remember once trying to pour some tea for both of them and spilling it all over the place. Alf said, "for heaven's sake, Vickie, pour the bloody tea before he scalds us all."'

Cohen features in one of the iconic photographs of the 1966 tournament. After England's win against Argentina, he tried to swap shirts with Alberto Gonzalez, only for Ramsey to step in and prevent it. Cohen never did get an Argentine shirt, but a week later he did have a World Cup winners medal. In fact, in addition to George, the Cohen family boasts another World Cup winner in Ben Cohen, who won the rugby union equivalent with England in 2003, and later took part in *Strictly Come Dancing*. Sadly Ben's father, Peter, younger brother of George, was attacked outside his nightclub in 2000 and died later in hospital.

So there is anguish in the Cohen family to list alongside achievement. However, an hour spent with George is enough to realise that he has a precious ability to keep things in perspective. Though still a regular visitor to Fulham's home matches, these days he prefers to discuss his grandchildren rather than his football career. His wife, Daphne, said simply, 'We did a lot of crying at the time, and then you have to move on. I am married to a brave and remarkable man.'

THE FRONT page story in The People on 12 April 1964 – involving Tony Kay, Peter Swan and 'Bronco Layne' – was not the first time the newspaper had revealed that football matches were being fixed. Other players from lower divisions had been named earlier, but these three were altogether bigger fish, and the match in question – Ipswich Town v Sheffield Wednesday in December 1962 – was a First Division fixture.

The ringleader of a series of betting coups, an ex-professional called Jimmy Gauld, had first approached Layne. He persuaded his club colleagues to join in and each had staked £50 on Wednesday to lose. Meanwhile, to increase the betting odds, Gauld had linked the match with two lower league games that he had also 'fixed', but the eventual return was poor. The Wednesday players, on top of their stake, received £100 – barely more than a fortnight's wages.

What none of them knew was that Gauld, who had already been exposed by the newspaper, had by then agreed to work for the People and help their reporter Michael Gabbert track down former 'customers'.

In all, ten players were tried at Nottingham Assizes. Not all received jail sentences but the mastermind Gauld was given four years, and Kay, Swan and Layne were each sentenced to four months imprisonment at Thorpe Arch open prison near Leeds. Mr Justice Lawton said: 'For £100, Kay has finished what is probably one of the greatest careers in football.' Within days of their release, the three men were banned for life by the FA.

In his autobiography, the then secretary of the Football League, Alan Hardaker, defended the use of secret tape recordings: 'I do not think they [the People] could have done the job any other way. I felt a little sorry for some of the smaller fish scooped up in the net. The heavyweights who were caught deserved all they got.'

Not everyone felt the same way. During the 1966 World Cup, a letter to The Times – signed by, among others, Matt Busby – argued that they had all been properly punished, and the case should be reviewed. It was not until 1972 that Swan's appeal against his lifetime ban was successful, and both he and Layne

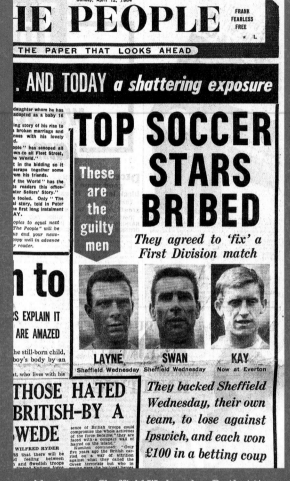

could return to Sheffield Wednesday. By that time their careers were almost at an end, though Swan managed a return to Wembley in 1975 – twenty-three years after his last appearance for England – as player-manager of FA Trophy winners Matlock Town.

Tony Kay never played league football again. Fifty years after the 'Sports Scandal of the Century', he shows little sign of slowing down. After a four-year self-imposed exile in Spain, and a life of low-wage manual labour, he now has a full-time job in a smart seaside restaurant and still does a gym session three times a week. Into his late seventies, he may well be the fittest man for his age in the country.

But then Kay always had a fire in him that both players and managers recognised and respected. He was at one time a fearless schoolboy goalkeeper, but switched to midfield and signed professional for Sheffield Wednesday in 1954. Hillsborough was a mere twenty-minute walk from his home.

Wednesday's pin-up at the time was Albert Quixall, already an England international. 'He was the golden boy and could do no wrong,' recalls Kay.

'I got in big trouble playing for the reserves against the first team for tackling him too hard. He had a real moan to the manager and I didn't forget. After he moved to Manchester United, they made him captain for the day against his old club. While we were tossing up I gave him a little bit of a slap to remind him who he was playing against.'

Nor did Kay let up when facing Pelé and Santos in a famous friendly in 1962: 'It didn't matter who we were playing, I got stuck in. Away from home, if I wasn't being booed, I thought I wasn't playing well.'

In December 1962, Harry Catterick – who had left Wednesday to manage Everton – tried to persuade Kay to make the same journey: 'The first time, he offered to double my wages to around £60 a week but I said no. I was happy living and playing in Sheffield. But he came back and, in addition to the wages, and a crowd bonus, he said there would be £2,000 in cash for me. A fortune in those days.'

Everton paid Wednesday almost £60,000, but Kay's arrival on Merseyside coincided with a winter freeze, leaving him sat on the sidelines for six weeks: 'Roy Vernon and Alex Parker took me out in Liverpool, but I told them I wasn't having a proper drink until I'd proved myself in my first match. We eventually played at Swindon in our all-white kit. After two minutes I slipped, fell on my arse and was head to toe in mud. Story of my life.'

Kay had already caught the eye of Alf Ramsey, playing for the England under-23s, and was selected for his first cap against Brazil in April 1963: 'Catterick called me into his office and said, "Congratulations on your call up for England. By the way you are not playing."'

The manager kept him back for an important First Division fixture, and soon, with the addition of Sheffield steel, Everton claimed the title for the first time since the war.

Ramsey selected Kay for England's summer tour, and he finally made his debut against Switzerland: 'We'd been in Bratislava and East Berlin, which were pretty depressing. When we arrived at the hotel in Switzerland, they produced cream cakes and scones, which we fell upon. It must have done some good. We won 8-1, and I scored with a good dig from near the halfway line.' Of the England manager, Kay recalled that, 'I liked Ramsey. Very honest with players, but quite shy really, with that funny way of talking. But I also liked Walter Winterbottom. I met him on a course in Lilleshall. Lovely man.'

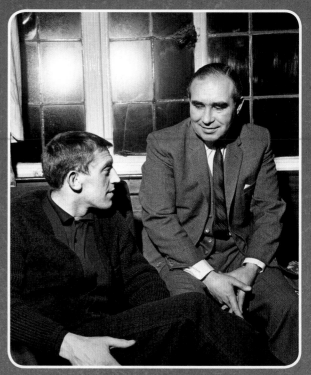

Kay remembers clearly how the fateful bet took place. 'Layne said he could get me two to one on Wednesday losing at Ipswich. I said we never win there, and gave him £50. If I'd bet on us to win I would probably have been all right. As is well known, the same paper which published the story also made me man of the match that day. Everton were victims, too, because they'd only had a season out of me for the money they'd paid. The club were very supportive, and let us keep the house for a while, but I wasn't allowed to train.'

Kay recalls meeting Gauld in his car and that during the trial, despite its quality, a recording of their conversation was ruled admissible in court: 'In the end prison wasn't too bad,' says Kay. 'The governor was a great bloke, mad on football, and a big Leeds supporter. I once tried to get him to take us to Elland Road when Everton were playing – in overcoats and a big hat over our faces! When we were due for release, he went out of his way to help us. The night before, about forty reporters had gathered outside the main gate, waiting for us to come out at 6 a.m. So he woke us up much earlier, and we walked across some fields to his house where he'd laid on a huge breakfast. We actually left from there.'

Almost as soon as the jail sentence finished, the FA imposed their ban on Kay and his two colleagues: 'That was the worst time, especially for my wife, Marina, and the four kids, and we split up not long afterwards. I really missed playing. Even when there was a chance I could go to America, FIFA put a stop to it.

'While I was suspended I'd started a recycling business, collecting cardboard from the docks. I tried to get back into it, but it didn't really work. I was skint, keeping bad company and getting more and more into trouble.

'A fella I knew had a diamond ring and said if I sold it for him I'd get a cut. I took it to Manchester, but it turned out it was a zircon. My dad told me the police were looking for me, so I just got the first plane out to Spain and stayed there for four years. Eventually I came back with a mate and borrowed

a car to go to a boxing match. We got stopped by the police, he was breathalysed, and when they found out who I was, I got done for the ring. It was a Bank Holiday weekend and I spent it locked up.'

Both in Spain, and on his return to England, however, Kay continued to play – with other ex-pros – in charity and other matches, under an assumed name: 'We called ourselves the Old Contemptibles and if people knew who I was they never let on. I had moved down to London by then and was working as a groundsman in Blackheath. I must have played in hundreds of matches, and only stopped when my knees gave in. Mind you I was sixty-two by then.'

In August 2002, Kay was persuaded to attend a parade of former players at Goodison Park. All week there had been rumours of his return to the club where, in less than sixty matches, he had left such an impression.

His partner, Becky Tallentire, author of a number of insightful books about Everton, recalls the occasion: 'It was such an emotional evening. No one was sure if Tony would turn up or not. He'd been away nearly forty years. Two by two, the players were introduced and then, at the very end, the tannoy announced his name and everyone went mad. I was in the stands, and he got his own Mexican wave as he walked round the pitch. People were crying and running down the touchlines trying to shake his hand or hug him. That's how it's been ever since round here. The Everton fans just love him.'

'I will never forget that night,' Kay adds. 'You can say what you like about Scousers, but I won't hear a word against them. They are loyal people and they don't forget you. I may be from Sheffield, but that night I felt I had finally come home.'

6: EXPERIMENTATION
AUGUST TO DECEMBER 1964

February 1957. Bobby Charlton rises above goalkeeper Willie Duff and Manchester United teammate Billy Whelan on the way to his first hat-trick in league football, against Charlton Athletic at The Valley.

FOR A SHORT TIME IN THE EARLY 1950S, THE SMALL PIT VILLAGE OF ASHINGTON IN NORTHUMBERLAND WITNESSED A SHARP SPIKE IN POPULATION.

The reason was nothing to do with the local mine whose seams of coal continued to provide the bulk of employment.

Instead, the increase was entirely due to the flock of soccer scouts who had beaten a path to the door of a small terraced house. Their target was a shy fifteen-year-old who not only hailed from a football family – his second cousin, Jackie Milburn, was a north-east icon – but on whom football's fairy godmother had been unduly generous.

Bobby Charlton was so talented a footballer as a schoolboy that there was never a chance of him pursuing another career. But in order that he fulfilled all that potential, and didn't fall by football's wayside, the godmother added an insurance policy. She entrusted his early career at Old Trafford to a coach who gave idle apprentices nightmares: a tough, pot-bellied, often foul-mouthed Welshman called Jimmy Murphy.

On the training ground, Murphy spent hours with the teenage Charlton. Together they worked on his passing, shooting and running with the ball. In *My Manchester United Years*, Charlton readily confessed to James Lawton the impact of Murphy: 'He was the most persistent and profound football influence I would ever know,' he recalled. 'He taught me that if you really want to show people you are a serious professional and not someone playing at it, you've got to find yourself space. You've got to work your balls off … he told me that the public will forgive you if you shoot and miss, but not if you have the chance to shoot and don't. He said

just hit it low and as hard as you can in the general direction of the goal.'

It helped, of course, if you were genuinely two-footed, with the ability to pass either side of a defender at speed. But Murphy's lessons were important in Charlton's development, too, and played a part in the pivotal moment of the 1966 finals. Carrying the ball from halfway in England's second match against Mexico, and preparing to shoot, Charlton heard only the voice of his mentor:

'Don't look up. Put your faith in the flight of the ball and let the goalie worry about where it's going to finish up.'

In Mexico's goal, Calderon had good cause to be worried and offered a speculative dive. He might honestly have saved the stain on his jersey as Charlton's right-foot shot flew past him from more than twenty-five yards. England were off and running.

Charlton's role as a deep-lying number nine in 1966 was actually the third edition of his England career. It had begun in April 1958, barely two months after he had been thrown into the snow on a Munich runway, still strapped to his seat, outside the crashed Elizabethan aircraft which claimed the lives of eight of his United teammates.

Selected at inside forward for his debut against Scotland at Hampden, he marked the occasion by scoring with a sumptuous volley. He retained his place for the friendly against Portugal – obliging him to miss United's European Cup semi-final against AC Milan the next day – and scored both England goals. The young man was now both box office and *Boy's Own* hero.

But England's next match was in Belgrade, where the Busby Babes had played their last match before the fatal crash. Not surprisingly the twenty-year-old had a poor game, though he was not alone as England conceded five goals without reply to Yugoslavia.

Charlton was dropped by Winterbottom and, despite a spirited press campaign for his recall, was only a travelling reserve in England's 1958 World Cup squad in Sweden. Regaining his place at the start of the following season, he was again England's hero when his diving header was enough to beat Scotland at Wembley in April 1959. The match marked Billy Wright's hundredth international; the next man to reach that landmark would be Charlton himself.

A home defeat by Sweden in October checked his progress, and the selection committee which had chosen him to play alongside Brian Clough promptly discarded them both. When he returned – again against the Scots at Hampden – it was in a new role on the left wing.

OVERLEAF | October 1964. Bobby Moore and Terry Neill lead out England and Northern Ireland for the Home International in Belfast. Behind Neill is George Best, who in only his third international inspired the Irish comeback.

Bobby Moore and wife Tina relaxing at home. In October 1964 Alf Ramsey was unhappy with Moore's attitude but retained him as England captain.

He had been persuaded to play there by his club manager, Matt Busby, and results were mixed. Charlton's performances matched those of the United team as a whole as the club recovered from Munich in the early 1960s. At times his talent could take him past a full back at will, allowing him both to create goals and to score spectacularly with either foot. At other times, to quote one journalist, it required a search party to establish that he was still on the field.

There were sublime moments for England also. In Chile in 1962, Charlton was voted the best outside left in the World Cup finals, and, as Winterbottom gave way to Ramsey, his role remained unchanged.

Charlton, however, still yearned for a return to inside forward. In the end, help was close at hand in the shape of a skinny seventeen-year-old, whose celebrity status would eventually eclipse even Charlton's, and embody the mix of football and fashion in the late 1960s.

George Best had made just one appearance for Manchester United when he was summoned from his family home in Belfast for a match against Burnley on 28 December 1963.

With Best rampant, United, who had been thrashed by the same opponents two days earlier, reversed the outcome at Old Trafford. Best became a permanent fixture on the left wing, and before the end of the season Matt Busby signed another winger, John Connelly – from Burnley.

The arrival of Best meant Charlton was now free to pursue a third coming for club and country. For the match against Northern Ireland in October 1964, he was selected alongside Gordon Milne in a midfield role, with Peter Thompson on the left wing. One newspaper said it was now 'Make or Break for Bobby the Schemer'. Ray Wilson, recently signed by Everton from Huddersfield, was injured and Bobby Thomson was again recalled into the side.

Charlton aside, what interested journalists most was that Ramsey had declined to name a captain. They speculated that Maurice Norman would replace Bobby Moore, who said only: 'I have not heard anything from Mr Ramsey and it is better that I make no comment.'

The truth was that the England manager's admiration for Moore as a player was matched by his doubts about him as a leader. Ramsey demanded the diligence of a school prefect; Moore – with Greaves and Budgie Byrne alongside – too often wanted to act the smart-arse at the back of the class. Following the escape to The Beachcomber in May there had been other instances on the summer tour where it appeared his captain preferred a couple of drinks to squad discipline. In the modern idiom, Ramsey wondered whether Moore was really 'on message'.

Ramsey was no innocent abroad. Alcohol was part of the football culture he'd grown up with; he knew players could let you down at times. But where England was concerned, Ramsey was on a mission. His squads were with him only for short intervals: was it too much to ask that those about to represent their country should behave responsibly?

The England manager's problem was that the society he'd grown up with was disappearing fast. Players in Ramsey's era – their careers at the mercy of club owners and managers – knew their place. With the wage cap now long gone, the mere fact of salary negotiation was driving a coach and horses through any notion of deference.

The 'swinging sixties' has become a tired and misleading phrase; they clearly didn't touch all, or at least not all at once. It was several years before they reached the likes of Rochdale. But the times were changing, and, as an American lyricist of the decade made clear, those in authority increasingly found that their sons – and their daughters – were beyond their command.

The entertainment business had led the way. In both film and popular music, a working-class background was becoming a virtue rather than an impediment to success. Michael Caine had no need of Ramsey's elocution lessons; there was no need to sound 'posh' to get on. Football, with its deep roots in working-class culture, followed closely.

Gordon Milne was aware how players' lives were looking up: 'When I joined Liverpool there were only three cars in the car park, and none of them belonged to the players. But then the salary change happened, and suddenly it was a great time to be young and single in the city. There was a club in Liverpool called the Royal Tiger where they would always look after us. Our night out was Wednesday. Everton went there on Tuesday. We knew Shirley Bassey

Following an England get-together in Derbyshire, Fred Pickering and Gordon Banks share a cup of tea with local workmen. Pickering scored five goals in three matches for England, but was one of many forwards who tried and failed to convince Alf Ramsey.

| Pat Jennings and his fellow defenders were powerless to prevent England scoring four first-half goals against Northern Ireland in Belfast. But in the end Ramsey's team were lucky to escape with a 4–3 win, ushering in a wave of criticism of the England manager.

and other stars of the time. We'd see The Beatles around town. Mind you, they weren't much interested in football.'

Further south, the change was even more marked for those with money in their pocket. Dominic Sandbrook, in his comprehensive history of the 1960s, *White Heat*, quotes historian Jerry White as saying that 'London's temples were now the boutique and discotheque … its high priests, the pop star, the fashion designer, the model and the photographer.' All featured in the publication which epitomised the age: the *Sunday Times* colour supplement, first published in February 1962.

Bobby Moore, tall and blond, with a fondness for the good life, fitted easily into these new surroundings and saw nothing wrong with enjoying himself. He told his biographer, Jeff Powell, 'I like a drink and as long as it's not to excess I feel better for it. But if you're seen holding a lager in this country people start shaking their heads and asking what happened to the clean-living sportsman.'

Ramsey would have fronted any queue of head-shakers. But back in Belfast, he and Moore had a frank discussion about the conduct required as captain. Not all fences were mended, and Moore was still keeping mum about a serious medical problem, but the two men reached agreement on one thing: Moore would remain as captain.

In place of Byrne, Ramsey had decided to give another chance to Fred Pickering up front. The Everton man was a throwback to the days when trams ruled city streets and the likes of Nat Lofthouse led England's attack. He had been converted from a full back by Blackburn Rovers, who had then sold him in March for £80,000. It was Pickering who put England ahead, and when Greaves completed his hat-trick after half an hour everything looked rosy. But in the second half things fell apart. The Irish, inspired by Best in only his third international, pulled three goals back. Two of them were scored by Swansea's Jimmy McLaughlin, who played on despite breaking two bones in his left hand.

The press reaction was brutal. It was one thing losing in Rio; hanging on for a 4–3 win in Belfast was quite another. 'Ninety minutes of shambles ought to be enough to end the eighteen-month reign of amiable Alfred,' said the *Mail*. The *Mirror* queried the effectiveness of Charlton and Milne in midfield and predicted the manager's response as anything but amiable: 'Ramsey will swing the axe. Shocked England must plan all over again for World Cup.'

Ramsey's chance to make changes came in a match against Belgium at Wembley on 21 October. The visitors were not expected to trouble England unduly, though they had beaten Brazil 5–1 in Brussels the previous year. Based on the Anderlecht team, their chief threat was Paul Van Himst, who in May had represented Europe – along with England's Wilson, Greaves and Charlton – in a match to celebrate the Danish FA's seventy-fifth anniversary.

Ramsey's axe turned out to be more precise than powerful. He left the defence alone but moved Peter Thompson to the right wing to give Alan Hinton a chance on the left. Hinton had not played since winning his only cap against France in 1962, but he had been in good form for Nottingham Forest since joining them in January

'IF YOU'RE SEEN HOLDING A LAGER IN THIS COUNTRY PEOPLE START SHAKING THEIR HEADS AND ASKING WHAT HAPPENED TO THE CLEAN-LIVING SPORTSMAN'

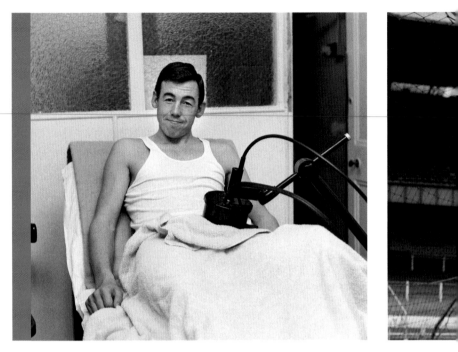

| With Gordon Banks (left) forced to pull out of England's international against Belgium, sixteen-year-old Billy Snasdall (centre) stands in for an England training session at Chelsea and Tony Waiters (right) for the actual match at Wembley.

from Wolves. Charlton was left out, and there was talk of a recall for Fulham's Johnny Haynes. Ramsey, though, preferred new lamps to old: inside Hinton he selected Terry Venables of Chelsea, the current leaders of the First Division.

Venables, like Ramsey, was born in Dagenham. Culturally, though, he was light years away from the world which the manager inhabited. The Chelsea captain, to an even greater extent than Moore, was one of a new breed of professionals: unafraid to speak his mind in public, and comfortable in the company of businessmen, actors and musicians. As a teenager Venables had sung with Joe Loss and his orchestra, and later in his career released a single.

The day before the Belgium match, Gordon Banks pulled out of a training session. The news had a knock-on effect for two other goalkeepers: sixteen-year-old Billy Snasdall, Chelsea's fourth choice, stood in for Banks and became the focus for photographers. Tony Waiters, meanwhile, replaced Banks for the match at Wembley.

The FA News report on the game professed itself 'pleasantly surprised by the tremendous improvement of this small but

enthusiastic football nation.' Gordon Milne, marking the slender Josef Jurion, who played in glasses, was less patronising: 'Quite honestly, Belgium murdered us.'

If it hadn't been for Waiters, the Belgians might have added to the goal they scored after twenty-two minutes. Though Pickering levelled, Van Himst was giving Norman and Moore a chasing and put the visitors ahead again before half-time. England were slow handclapped in the second half by the 45,000-strong crowd, but twenty minutes from time Hinton's cross was deflected past Nicolay, making the final score 2–2.

The post-mortems of the game were predictable. Less so was the result of an extraordinary general meeting of the Football League on the day of the match. A vote of no confidence in the management committee – for agreeing a deal with BBC Television – was defeated. *Match of the Day* had begun life a couple of months earlier on 22 August 1964, when edited highlights of just one game were transmitted at 6.30 p.m. on BBC2, then available only in the London area.

Kenneth Wolstenholme introduced the show, and was also the commentator on Liverpool's win over Arsenal, with Roger Hunt scoring the first goal.

Multi-camera coverage and the use of videotape was a step up from the old days of film, though action replays were still some way off. The iconic programme, which currently attracts a good deal more viewers than the 20,000 who saw the first edition, recently celebrated its fiftieth anniversary.

On 11 November, seven days before England's next game against Wales, it was reported in the press that, 'Bobby Moore has been operated on for an injured groin. He will not play again for two months'. Only the second part was true; Moore's injury was in fact testicular cancer and he had undergone surgery two days earlier. The condition had troubled the West Ham captain for some time. Now, when properly diagnosed and treated, the exact nature of the problem was kept a close secret by his family, and revealed only after Moore's death in 1993.

Even if Ramsey had known the details, he would be the last one to admit it. He had his own problems, of which naming another captain was one. He told the waiting press that he was still experimenting: 'I must go on trying players. I have until the end of the season and then I must settle on a pool of players for 1966.'

His initial selection for the Welsh match included a new half back line. Milne was left out in favour of Mike Bailey, and, as things turned out, would not play for England again. Ron Flowers replaced Norman and was made captain, with a new cap, Gerry Young of Sheffield Wednesday, coming in for Moore.

In attack, Ramsey again showed itchy fingers. Pickering was stood down after a hat-trick in his first international and a goal in each of his other two games. His replacement, Frank Wignall of Nottingham Forest, had resurrected his career after being sold by Everton and a week after England's match against Belgium he had scored a hat-trick for the Football League against the Irish League.

The League matches, like the under-23 England games, allowed the England manager room to experiment outside the full

Terry Venables travelling on public transport in London. The Chelsea captain, like Bobby Moore, typified a new breed of professional, no longer the humble servant of his employer. Named in the World Cup 40, Venables moved to Spurs in May 1966, but never added to the two England caps he won in 1964.

| (Top) Frank Wignall scored both goals on his England debut, but against the Dutch (bottom) once again Jimmy Greaves rescued England, equalising with just four minutes left.

internationals. But there were further concerns for Ramsey when both Venables and Greaves were injured and had to be replaced by Byrne and the ever-patient Hunt. With hindsight, this moment may have been the lowest point in the three-year campaign to win the World Cup. One newspaper neatly summed up the manager's lack of options: 'Mr Ramsey is short of talent, and short of time.'

With Wembley less than half full, England beat Wales 2–1, both goals being scored by Wignall. 'England', said the *Daily Mirror*, 'have found a centre forward who plays with purpose, who moves with the mobility of a man who knows what it's all about.'

The Forest man kept his place for England's final match of 1964: to celebrate the seventy-fifth anniversary of the Netherlands FA. The previous meeting of the teams in 1946 had finished 8–2 to England, but the Dutch – like the Belgians – had learned quickly.

For the match in Amsterdam, Young was out with an injury and so his club colleague Vic Mobley was stood by. In the end there were recalls for Maurice Norman in defence – in what turned out to be his final match for England – and for Greaves, Venables and Charlton. In midfield Alan Mullery, who had missed England's summer tour, was finally awarded his first cap.

The game was played in a cold and windy Olympic Stadium on 9 December. The Dutch adapted better to the conditions and went ahead in the second half with a tremendous strike by their left winger, Moulijn. It looked to be enough until, with four minutes left, Mullery and Venables combined to release Greaves to do what he had done for most of his football life – turn the last defender and leave the goalkeeper helpless.

Back home in Ipswich for Christmas, the England manager could look back on a calendar year in which his team had on occasions shown promise. Twelve matches played and only three defeats – two of them in the heat and humidity of South America – was not exactly a bad record. But too many of his squad seemed to flower in one match and flounder in the next.

Peter Thompson had looked world-class in Brazil, but was prone to disappear at times. Budgie Byrne, for different reasons, had almost disappeared altogether since the summer, and the search for a partner for Greaves would go on.

As for a creative force behind the front players, a quarterback if you like, Ramsey had seen something others had missed: 'I knew months, even years, before the World Cup,' he confided to journalist Arthur Hopcraft in 1968, 'that Bobby Charlton would have a number nine on his back.' That move, so crucial in the end for England, would take time to bear fruit. It would require not only a change in personnel but also a different and innovative team formation.

ROGER HUNT

LIKE HIS England colleague Ray Wilson, Roger Hunt was fortunate that he had a family business to enter when he chose to leave football, and never had to experience the fickleness of football management. Had he done so, he would have surely found a shortage of players like himself.

Adaptable and diligent, Hunt was a manager's dream, whether playing for the extrovert Bill Shankly at Liverpool, or the more withdrawn Alf Ramsey with England.

Both managers knew that in Hunt they had a man who would never hide, would run all day to make a poor pass into a good one, and a good one into a goal. He may have lacked the impish skills and finishing touch of his rival Jimmy Greaves, but his record of 245 league goals for Liverpool may never be beaten: eighteen in thirty-four matches for England is pretty good going.

At twenty-one, Hunt was a late starter in the professional game, after leaving the army: 'My first trial was a disaster, and at the end of it my father said I should forget about football and join his business. But Joe Fagan encouraged me to keep working, and I got into the first team eventually. That was in 1959, and Liverpool were still in the Second Division, but two months later Bill Shankly arrived and everything just took off.'

Hunt's ambition was to win the FA Cup, something Liverpool had never achieved. He had no thoughts of playing for England. However, in April 1962, the year Liverpool were promoted, he was selected by Walter Winterbottom for a match against Austria. He scored on his debut, but since the BBC commentator referred to the goal as 'a great header by Ralph Hunt', he was clearly still struggling for recognition. He travelled to Chile with the England World Cup squad, but was not chosen for any of the four games.

A year later, Alf Ramsey picked him to play in East Germany, when he scored again, but his displays for England were always being measured against those of Greaves: 'Before the World Cup, when I did get a game, it seemed I was being blamed because Jimmy wasn't playing. There was also a bit of a north versus south thing in the papers. Bob Paisley used to think there was more chance of being picked if you played well in London.'

Ramsey, of course, never allowed the press, or anyone else, to influence his selection. But, as he gradually took the wrapping off his 4-3-3 formation, he found in Hunt one of the key ingredients to make it work.

Liverpool's pre-eminence, winning the league in 1964 and 1966, and the FA Cup in 1965, when Hunt scored their first goal, was based on a classic 4-2-4: 'I was an old-fashioned inside forward, and we had two great wingers in Cally and Peter Thompson. But Alf wanted to do things differently. I remember when we played in Spain. It was strange not seeing anyone on the wings. I wondered how it would work, but in the end we won easily. Much of the time, especially when Geoff came in, there would be just two of us up front. It was hard work. You'd be outnumbered, and not getting a lot of the ball. In the final I hardly had a kick in the first fifteen minutes, and dropped back, but Alf told me at half-time to stay up and challenge their sweeper.'

Earlier Hunt had hidden his disappointment at being allotted the number twenty-one shirt, which appeared to signal he would be a reserve in the finals. However, he scored a fine goal in the last warm-up match in Poland and was picked for the opening match against Uruguay. He then scored three times in the next two group matches. Even now he is asked – 'about four days a week' – about the final against West Germany, and why he didn't follow up and score when Hurst's shot hit the bar in extra time: 'I thought the ball was about a foot over the line, and turned away. But if you look at the film you can see the ball then bounced high and at an angle before Weber knocked it out for a corner.'

Hunt played his last game for England in January 1969, and told Ramsey he wanted to retire from international football: 'I always liked Alf. If you were doing your stuff for him, whatever your club form, he would stick with you. But I didn't want to be involved in another World Cup when I'd have been thirty-two anyway. Shanks was also breaking up the Liverpool side of the 1960s and I moved to Bolton, the team I used to support. I also got involved in the haulage business which my father and uncle had started. I missed the game to start with, but I was busy at work and it gradually wore off.'

Looking back, Hunt is proud of playing all six matches in 1966: 'That's what some people forget. They have never forgiven me for taking Jimmy's place in the final, even if I didn't. They were great times. Before we played Everton in the Charity Shield match that year, they showed off the FA Cup, we had the League Championship trophy and Ray Wilson and I paraded with the World Cup.

'Mind you, Shanks had the last word. After winning the World Cup, I had a couple of days at home and then reported back for training with Liverpool. All he said to me was, "Well done, son, but we've got more important things to do now!"'

7: REVELATION
JANUARY TO JUNE 1965

I Nobby Stiles in typical aggressive mood on his debut for England against Scotland at Wembley. Much criticised for his lack of elegance in midfield, Stiles fulfilled a vital role for England. 'My job', he said, 'is to win the ball, and give it to Bobby Charlton.'

IN FEBRUARY 1965, MANCHESTER UNITED'S NOBBY STILES WAS A WORRIED MAN.

After months of struggling for a regular first-team slot at Old Trafford, Stiles had finally found a place alongside Bill Foulkes in United's defence. So much so that the previous occupant of the position and his main rival, Maurice Setters, had been transferred to Stoke the previous November. Matt Busby's United were locked in a battle with Chelsea and Leeds for the championship – a title they had not won since the 'Babes' had triumphed in 1957. A vital fixture, away at Sunderland on Tuesday 24 February, was looming for Stiles and colleagues. But this was also the date of an under-23 match against the Scots, for which Stiles had also been selected. Stiles knew this was a chance, perhaps the only one, to force himself into Ramsey's thinking for the World Cup. The previous Saturday Busby had made his position clear: he expected the young man to play at Roker Park. But in a subsequent phone call the following day Stiles found the courage to tell his boss he would be in Aberdeen, in England colours, on the night in question.

Reliving the dilemma, Stiles told his biographer, James Lawton, in *After the Ball* that, 'For once I had stood up to Busby. A little of the awe I had brought to United as a schoolboy slipped away. I was no longer a boy; I was a husband and father and a footballer in the running for the World Cup.' Playing further forward than his usual club position, Stiles impressed Ramsey in Aberdeen with his ability to choose the right option: not only when to go in hard but – like an intelligent sheepdog – when to steer opponents away from

ABOVE | Wilf McGuinness, who assured Alf Ramsey that Nobby Stiles would certainly not hold back when facing his club colleague Denis Law at Wembley.

goal and into places of safety. Stiles helped shut the Scots out in a goalless draw. United, without his defensive capabilities, lost 1–0.

Two months later, Stiles' decision to stand up to Busby bore fruit and he was rewarded with his first full cap, also against Scotland. According to Wilf McGuinness, then a coach at Old Trafford but also assistant to Ramsey with the under-23 team, there was one final question that was settled for Stiles' selection: 'Alf asked me if Nobby would be as hard as he was in the under-23 game when facing his United club colleague Denis Law at Wembley. All I said was: "no f*****g danger."'

If the choice of Stiles was still something of a surprise, Ramsey ensured reporters and photographers had an undemanding day by selecting Bobby Charlton's elder brother to play centre half.

Jack Charlton was nearly thirty, but had been a defensive rock for Leeds all season as they challenged for both cup and league. As

'WHEREAS BOBBY WAS SHY AND UNASSUMING, JACK WAS LOUD AND CONFIDENT IN HIS OWN ABILITY'

a young man Jack had been spared his brother's gifts, and at one time seemed more likely to be a miner than a footballer. However, he had joined Leeds in 1952, and after National Service gained a regular first-team place when John Charles, a legend at the club, moved to centre forward.

Whereas Bobby was shy and unassuming, Jack was loud and confident in his own ability. But it was only after Don Revie took over as manager of Leeds in 1961 that the tall, gangly youth made the most of his size and strength and became the model professional.

Alan Peacock, who joined Leeds in time to get a Second Division championship medal in 1964, remembers his teammate's attitude well: 'Jack was a good player but he always wanted to tell everyone else what to do. And he was never wrong! At corners he would shout at all of us to mark, but if it was his man that scored it was never his fault! We had a good young side, and most of them were frightened of him. I remember him losing his temper with Gary Sprake and chasing him round the back of the goal with the game still going on … Don used to tell Jack he was never going to be as good as his brother Bobby. If he thought that for a minute, he'd be out of the team. In the end he listened, and showed us all what he could do.'

Having played with Stiles in a Football League match in March 1965, Charlton was also chosen to make his debut for the full England team. This meant demotion for the Spurs pair of Alan Mullery and Maurice Norman. Mullery's time would come again, but for the likeable and loyal Norman, exactly one year older than Jack Charlton, it was the end of the road: the loss of his England place followed on from losing his club place; a few months later, in November 1965, he suffered a broken leg in a friendly and was forced to retire.

As well as bringing in new personnel, Ramsey was also trialling a new tactical formation for the side. At an England practice session in February, Ramsey had experimented by sending out his senior players in a 4-3-3 formation against the under-23 team and been delighted with the result. The senior midfield of Douglas, Byrne and

OVERLEAF | March 1965. Norman Hunter (left) and Jack Charlton celebrate their call up for the Football League team. A month later Charlton, at almost thirty years of age, made his full international debut for England. Hunter's first cap came in December, as a substitute against Spain in Madrid.

Eastham had utterly confounded the younger opposition, who had expected to face the more usual 4-2-4.

The England manager was on to something. The new system would need further manipulation, but could solve the two main problems with 4-2-4: the first was that, with just two players in midfield, there was the difficulty in winning enough possession; the second, now that most teams employed four defenders, was that wingers were more tightly marked and could be almost redundant at times.

Ramsey was not against wingers as such. He had played with and against the very best, including Stanley Matthews, who, astonishingly, had recently played his last First Division match at the age of fifty. Unfortunately for the England manager, however, the most effective – and younger – examples were either Welsh

(Cliff Jones), Scottish (Willie Henderson) or Irish (George Best). Without such riches, Ramsey required his wingers to be flexible – to do more than just hug the touchline before entering the fray. He felt they should track back if necessary, share the burden of the build-up, and – like Jimmy Leadbetter at Ipswich – make the full back uneasy about leaving his comfort zone.

Against Scotland on 10 April, Ramsey spread his bets. Instead of a simple 4-2-4 he allowed Bobby Charlton to leave his left-wing post for a midfield role alongside Stiles and Byrne. Up front he would choose only one out-and-out winger, Peter Thompson, to play alongside Greaves. The third member of the attacking line was yet another new centre forward in Barry Bridges. Bridges was one of a number of young Chelsea players to have caught the eye of the England manager. A former schoolboy and youth international, Bridges had made his first team debut – alongside another seventeen-year-old, Bobby Tambling – in 1959, but in the 1964–65 season had contributed hugely to Chelsea's attempt to win all three domestic competitions.

The Scots were favourites to win at Wembley, but for thirty-five minutes it was England in the ascendant, leading 2–0 through Charlton and Greaves. Then a mistake by Banks gifted Law a goal, and any assessment of England's new look was made irrelevant by injuries: first to Ray Wilson, and then more seriously to Byrne, who, in the continued absence of substitutes, had taken Wilson's place at left back. Down to nine fit men, with Bobby Charlton now playing at full back, England hung on for a 2–2 draw. His brother Jack, alongside Bobby Moore, had performed miracles. The press were full of praise, too, for Nobby Stiles, with one report claiming that, 'Nobby Stiles, his spirit spreading through the side like a forest fire, was a hero from the start.'

With Stiles patrolling in front of the back four, the new defensive line had faced difficult circumstances and had not been found wanting. From now on the litany of Banks, Cohen, Wilson, Stiles, Charlton (Jack) and Moore would be Ramsey's first choice – up to and including the World Cup final itself. All would be required for England's next game against Hungary on 5 May and for the summer

tour of Yugoslavia, West Germany and Sweden. However, club commitments in Europe were beginning to disrupt Ramsey's choice of players: Liverpool faced Internazionale of Milan in the semi-final of the European Cup; West Ham had already reached the Cup Winners' Cup final; Manchester United required their players for the Fairs Cup, still only at the quarter-final stage.

Before that, some domestic issues had to be resolved. The championship went to Manchester United, winning on goal average from Leeds United (the last time this method was required). The teams finished ahead of Chelsea; manager Tommy Docherty, with two games left, sent home from Blackpool captain Terry Venables, Barry Bridges and six other players for breaking a club curfew.

Leeds were also runners-up in the FA Cup to Liverpool. Gordon Milne missed the final through injury, and Gerry Byrne broke his collarbone in the opening minutes at Wembley. 'You'll never meet a tougher guy than Gerry,' recalls Milne, 'How he managed to stay on the pitch let alone finish the game I'll never know. Three days later we were asked to parade the FA Cup round the pitch together before the [European Cup] semi-final against Inter. After about ten minutes my arm was aching, and I was begging Gerry to let us put it down.

I April 1965. Disaster for England as first Ray Wilson (left) and then Johnny Byrne (centre) are injured in the match with Scotland. With England down to nine fit men, the match ended in a 2–2 draw and (right) a handshake between Denis Law and Bobby Moore.

But the place was going mad, and Gerry, with his arm in a sling and obviously in great pain, would not stop.'

The Hungary match was promoted as a chance for England to avenge the 6–3 defeat suffered by Ramsey and company in 1953, even though some key personnel were missing from the squad: Bobby Charlton was unfit, Eastham returned for the injured Byrne, and Connelly was chosen for the first time since Ramsey's first match in Paris. In the end, the match proved a tepid affair, decided by a solitary Greaves' goal.

For the summer tour eighteen players were selected and one of them in particular was desperate to play. As a boy Alan Ball had dreamt of becoming a professional, but his small frame meant early rejection slips from both Wolves and Bolton Wanderers.

Ball, however, had drive and determination to burn, not to mention the belief of his father, Alan Ball Senior, that he would make the grade. Ball's father had played at lower-league level, and was described by his son as 'my mentor, coach, adviser, critic, psychologist, disciplinarian and caring father.'

Faced with this family onslaught, it was Blackpool who surrendered first. They took Ball Junior on to the ground staff at

May 1965. Hungary's goalkeeper Gelei was beaten only once, by a Jimmy Greaves goal, in the match at Wembley. England's win was the first of four successive matches against continental opposition, none of which, thanks to the new defensive line up, ended in defeat.

Bloomfield Road. Ball's jobs included cleaning the boots of Stanley Matthews, a task which – to the shock of all who heard it – did not prevent the apprentice swearing at the great man for refusing to run for a pass in a practice match.

Ball's freshness and fearlessness on the pitch took him into the first team, then on to the England under-23s and eventually to a full cap. According to Ball, 'Alf Ramsey just came up to me the day before the match in Belgrade and said, "I think it's about time you made your debut for your country, don't you?"'

Ball for Eastham was England's only change for the match in Belgrade. The Yugoslavs, who had beaten England 5–0 on their previous visit, scored early, but Bridges equalised from a well-worked corner and from then on England took charge. The defence was again rock solid, with Terry Paine dropping deeper when required to support Ball, already doing the work of two men in midfield.

If the performance was good, the one in Nuremburg on 12 May was even better, especially since Ramsey had less than a full deck from which to choose: Stiles and Connelly were required by Manchester United for their match with Strasbourg; Thompson, by Liverpool for the second leg against Inter; Greaves, meanwhile, had a minor injury and was left out. Ramsey chose this match to experiment further with a 4-3-3 formation, playing Flowers, Ball and Eastham in midfield and Paine up front alongside two debutants – Mick Jones of Sheffield United and Everton's Derek Temple. Jones was the latest in a long line of centre forwards tried by Ramsey. The form of one of the earlier contenders, Frank Wignall, had rather deserted him since Christmas, and in any case he had broken a leg in an end-of-season County Cup final.

Germany, or even West Germany, had failed to beat England in any previous meeting. The record was preserved by Paine's winning goal, created by Temple. It turned out to be Temple's only cap. Though he failed to make England's final squad the following summer, he did play in a Wembley final in 1966, scoring the winning goal – after an error by Gerry Young – in the FA Cup final against Sheffield Wednesday. Interestingly, with fourteen months to go, the Germans fielded only four players who would go on to play in the World Cup

'I THINK IT'S ABOUT TIME YOU PLAYED FOR YOUR COUNTRY, DON'T YOU?'

OVERLEAF | Alan Ball in a cobbled street near his parents' home in Walkden, Lancashire. The young Blackpool forward was an outstanding success on England's summer tour in 1965. After his debut against Yugoslavia, he kept his place against West Germany and scored his first goal for his country against Sweden.

final; England fielded six. For Ball, born during 'Victory in Europe' week in 1945, victory in Nuremburg came on his twentieth birthday.

Against Sweden in Stockholm on 16 May he followed this up by scoring his first goal for England in a 2–1 win. The returning John Connelly got the winner in the easiest of the three tour games. Indeed, the only scare came before the match when Stiles' lens fluid went missing. Frantic phone calls resulted in Mary, daughter of FA secretary Denis Follows, buying the required solution late at night in Piccadilly, and BEA flying it out on the morning of the match.

Although the tour was over, the season was not. Stiles, Ball and Jones went on to join the under-23 tour of Europe: Ball played all three matches, in the last of which he was sent off against Austria on 2 June.

For several of the players there were the European cup competitions to complete. Three days after the Sweden match Bobby Moore lifted another trophy at Wembley as West Ham, minus the injured Budgie Byrne, won the Cup Winners' Cup final in style. Liverpool's Hunt and Thompson were less fortunate, losing their semi-final to Inter in dubious circumstances. The Manchester United trio of Stiles, Connelly and Bobby Charlton, by contrast, lost in their Fairs Cup semi-final play-off against Ferencvaros – on 16 June!

There was also further work for Ramsey to do. In a throwback to the Winterbottom era, the team manager was obliged to submit a report on the England tour to the FA's international committee. One can only imagine Ramsey's enthusiasm for such a task. Not surprisingly, the report contained few insights and was content merely to criticise the below-par performance of all three opponents – and the lack of England goals scored from chances created.

For all the England players it had been a long old season, but the next would be even longer: the World Cup finals were not due to start until 11 July. The England team had qualified as hosts, and would start among the favourites; off the field, other teams were already in place to ensure that the tournament, whether England were successful or not, was managed properly – and made a profit.

JACK CHARLTON

ONE EVENING when the two of them found themselves alone in a hotel bar, Jack Charlton asked Alf Ramsey why he had selected him for England in the first place. His reply was nothing if not forthright. 'Well, Jack,' said Ramsey, 'I have a pattern of play in my mind, and I choose the players to fit that pattern. They may not necessarily be the best players.'

Later he explained to Charlton that he picked him because he did the simple things well and because 'you don't trust Bobby Moore'. By that Ramsey meant that Charlton's defensive antennae were first class; that if the more cultured Moore moved forward with the ball, Charlton was already weighing up the consequences if he lost it, and was covering for him.

Charlton would go on to admit that, 'Alf was a difficult man to know. I'm not sure he liked me much because I was always arguing. But I learned a lot from

him.' Ramsey's analysis of the tall, awkward centre half may not have been entirely flattering, but he never underestimated his contribution, or his record. In thirty-seven internationals for England, Charlton lost only twice, including one when he himself was injured early in the match, and left to hobble on the wing.

Jack Charlton is two years older, and a good deal more outgoing than his brother Bobby. But it was the younger sibling who was bequeathed the footballing gifts. At one stage in his career, it seemed unlikely that Jack would set the city of Leeds alight, let alone play for England. He had been given his first team debut in 1953 as a seventeen-year-old, and when the club's idol John Charles was moved up front, Charlton took his place at centre half. Leeds won promotion in 1956, but Charles was sold a year later. Soon the club was back in the Second Division and in danger of dropping still further. Charlton had returned from National Service earlier, and by his own admission was causing aggravation to all, including Don Revie, the latest manager to try to restore the club's reputation. 'I was in limbo,' recalled Charlton in his autobiography, 'with a club that wasn't going anywhere. I didn't consider myself a particularly good player. I was just a young pro with a very famous brother who was making headlines at the time. Don said later I was one of the most awkward customers he'd had the misfortune to meet.'

Bill Shankly tried to sign him for Liverpool, and at one stage he seemed certain to join his brother Bobby at Manchester United. But Matt Busby dallied, and the rebel – for perhaps the only time in his life – backed off and signed a fresh contract with Leeds. All this time, Charlton – like a teenage tearaway doing charity work on the quiet – had become interested in coaching, regularly attending FA courses at Lilleshall with the likes of Bobby Robson, Lawrie McMenemy and Dave Sexton. Once he had attained the necessary badges, he began coaching in the Leeds area to supplement his club wages, but his experience at Lilleshall helped shape his career.

Charlton said later: 'Almost every player who was successful as a manager had been there. Those that had not – like my brother and Bobby Moore – never really made it as a manager.' Leeds too reaped the benefit. From being the troublemaker, Charlton now found himself as one of the senior players among a talented litter of youngsters like Billy Bremner, Terry Cooper and Norman Hunter: 'Someone had to help them. My idea was to do as little as possible on the field, and have a great game!'

With Don Revie's firm hand on the wheel, Charlton and his colleagues became a team to be feared, winning promotion back to the First Division in 1964, and finishing runners up in both cup and league the following season. 'We were tough customers,' admitted Charlton. 'It was all for one and one for all. If you kicked me, I wouldn't kick you back but someone else would. Later we changed our style, and played some wonderful football, but we were never forgiven for those early years.'

Charlton was almost thirty when the England call came. He and Nobby Stiles made their debuts together against Scotland in April 1965 and were Ramsey's first choice for two years. Charlton believed the pace of international football, compared with the helter-skelter of the first division, suited him: 'If I wasn't involved in a tackle, I found it quite easy. It wasn't a case of having more time on the ball, more that there was always someone there to give it to.'

Only one forward, the gangly Portugal centre forward Torres, caused Charlton any real problems during the 1966 finals. Late in the game, after his brother Bobby had scored two goals for England, Jack deliberately handled a Torres attempt, giving away a penalty. Though Eusebio scored it, retribution might have been worse: under today's rules, Charlton would have been sent off and missed the final.

Four years later, Charlton travelled to Mexico as reserve to Brian Labone, and played his final international in England's group match against Czechoslovakia. His last and 628th league match for Leeds took place in April 1973. By then he was nearly thirty-eight, and clearly management material. In his first season he took Middlesbrough back into the First Division and was preferred to Bill Shankly as Manager of the Year. He later had spells at Sheffield Wednesday and Newcastle. In 1986 he was appointed manager of the Republic of Ireland, and guided them to two World Cup and one European Championship finals, which included a memorable win over England in Stuttgart. Like Ramsey, Charlton picked a team to fit the way he wanted to them to play, launching attacks from deep and causing alarm to defenders unused to being harried near their own corner flags. They were memorable times for the nation, which rewarded him with Irish citizenship in 1996. Though football has given him a good living, Jack Charlton has always had a passion for the countryside, and for country pursuits. As a boy, growing up during the war years, he hunted rabbits and helped his father keep pigs, which served the family well fed in times of rationing. In retirement, he is probably most at ease with a fishing rod in his hands. One former colleague recalls him fondly: 'Jack was some character. Knew better than anyone in the club, and never lost an argument. You could hear him a mile away, but you could smell him too! That car of his was always full of cigarette butts and fishing gear – waders, rods, the lot. And in the boot these big cans of maggots!'

8: ORGANISATION
JULY 1965 TO JUNE 1966

September 1965. The World Cup headquarters at White City in west London where staff checked thousands of ticket applications. The cheapest ten-match season ticket, which guaranteed a place at the final on 30 July, could be purchased for less than four pounds.

FIFA AWARDED THE FOOTBALL ASSOCIATION THE RIGHT TO STAGE THE 1966 WORLD CUP FINALS AT THEIR CONGRESS IN ROME IN AUGUST 1960.

During the meeting there had been criticism of the FA for their support of the all-white South African FA, but in the end the voting was 34–27 in favour of England. The runner-up was West Germany.

The fact that the 1966 World Cup was to be held for the first time in the country where football was invented was greeted with a distinct lack of enthusiasm by the English press at the time. It was still very much the cricket season during the Rome meeting, and so, while ample coverage was given to an opening partnership of 290 by Pullar and Cowdrey in the test match at The Oval, *The Times* donated just four paragraphs to the World Cup vote.

For obvious reasons the organising of the World Cup in England needed to be divorced from the day-to-day activities of the FA. In September 1963, a separate headquarters was set up at the White City stadium in West London where one of the matches was due to be played.

Although only sixteen teams would qualify for the finals (compared with thirty-two in Brazil 2014), eight grounds would be required to host the thirty-two matches. FIFA stipulated that all World Cup pitches should be 115 yards long and 75 yards wide. This ruled out Arsenal's ground at Highbury, which was found to be a few yards short of the required length. Goodison Park had to be expensively lengthened and widened before being accepted, while one of the original choices in the North East, St James' Park, was replaced by Middlesbrough's Ayresome Park, because of contractual difficulties regarding the lease of the Newcastle ground from the local council.

An even bigger headache was money. FIFA in those days was not awash with cash; the World Cup sponsorship and marketing programme it now enjoys was still some years away, meaning almost all the financial risk was laid at the feet of the host nation. In the UK, the financial situation was little better: the organising committee failed to find any sponsor for its ticket brochure, despite it being sent out to 130 countries.

Nor, at first, was government help forthcoming. As Dominic Sandbrook makes clear in *White Heat*, when Harold Wilson became prime minister in October 1964, he had no idea that the World Cup was about to be played in England. It was not until the end of May 1965 that Denis Howell, the former referee and now the minister for sport, was able to announce that the FA would receive half a million pounds towards the upgrade of stadium facilities. For many clubs, if the sum was not too little, it was already too late because work could not be completed in time for the start of the new season.

Ticket sales were therefore crucial to the success of the event. After much discussion about price and availability, it was decided that creating a 'season ticket' – enabling fans to watch six group matches, a quarter-final, a semi-final, the third-place match and the final – would deliver the best results. The most expensive ticket for the ten matches was £25. 15s., while a standing season ticket was available for £3. 17s. 6d (around £450 and £70 in today's money).

There was no money either for newspaper advertising. Instead the committee put their faith in a poster campaign, and the image of a little lion in a Union Jack shirt, known as World Cup Willie. Willie was launched in July 1965 and was licensed to more than one hundred companies – producers of everything from bath mats to beer glasses, car stickers to cuff links. There was also a World Cup Willie song, sung by Lonnie Donegan. What was little known at the time was that the name for the lion derived from the nickname given by organising staff to their chief administrative officer, Ken Willson. Though he later received the MBE for his work on the event, he was not the recipient of any World Cup royalties!

ABOVE | September 1965. Ron Springett, back in the England team for the first time since Alf Ramsey's first match in charge, poses with other members of the squad while training at Stamford Bridge.

There were now just twelve months to go before the start of the tournament. The England team would have eight games before Alf Ramsey was obliged to name his final twenty-two players. The squad would then undertake a further four-match tour before the opening match of the finals on 11 July.

The first international of the new season, on 2 October, was against Wales in Cardiff. Ramsey retained Paine and Connelly in a traditional 4-2-4, but yet again Jimmy Greaves had a new partner. This time the centre-forward role went to Alan Peacock, whose last cap had come in Walter Winterbottom's final match – also against Wales.

Tall and straight-backed, Peacock had blossomed since leaving Middlesbrough. However, he had damaged a cruciate ligament in a

WORLD CUP

JULY 11 to 30
1966
ENGLAND

match for Leeds in East Berlin – an injury that was to have long-term repercussions.

'Of all the places to do it', recalled Peacock. 'They didn't want to leave me in hospital in the east. But when we got to Checkpoint Charlie I had to walk around these barriers to get into West Berlin. I was in semi-plaster and in agony, but eventually I got the plane back to Leeds. In those days you were told to carry on. I remember fracturing a cheekbone just before going to Chile, but just got on with it. It was the same with my knee. I couldn't turn very well, but I got myself really fit again, and was scoring goals, but to be honest I was never quite right after the knee injury.'

As well as Peacock up front, Bobby Charlton was restored in midfield. With Gordon Banks missing the first two months of

LEFT | FA secretary Denis Follows with the official mascot World Cup Willie, which was licensed to more than one hundred companies and helped the organisation make a substantial profit.

RIGHT | There was also a recall for the match against Wales for Alan Peacock, now of Leeds United. A long-term knee injury, however, meant his season came to an end after Christmas.

the season with a broken wrist, there was a recall in goal for Ron Springett, whose previous international had been Ramsey's first in Paris. In the *Daily Express*, Eric Cooper predicted a 5–1 win for

England, and was suitably critical when the match finished 0–0: 'Wales did England a service by making my forecast a flop. Plain old-fashioned football showed that, after three years under Alf Ramsey, England haven't even got a team working in unison, let alone a pattern, 4-2-4 or otherwise.'

Things were about to get worse. On 20 October, Austria, a side who had failed to qualify for the 1966 finals, became only the third overseas team to beat England at Wembley.

Ramsey had selected the team which drew in Cardiff, except with Bridges replacing an unfit Peacock. After Bobby Charlton put England ahead early on, his brother Jack headed against the bar and Greaves hit a post. But in a frantic second half, Austria equalised, conceded a goal to England's Connelly, then scored twice more to win the match in the last fifteen minutes.

The winning goal by Fritsch, his second, was accidentally left out in the highlights on ITV, whose viewers thought the match had ended 2–2. But the faces dipped in egg belonged to England.

In the press criticism that followed, Greaves was described by

| October 1965. Goals by Manchester United's Bobby Charlton (left) and John Connelly (centre) put England ahead against the unfancied Austrians. But the visitors fought back to win the match (right) and provide further ammunition for Ramsey's critics.

the *Daily Mail* as 'a pale spasmodic shadow' and the old arguments about the Spurs striker were revisited. Greaves was unquestionably the finest goalscorer of his generation and could make fools of his critics by changing the course of a match with a single strike. Four days before the Wembley match, he had run through five Manchester United defenders to score a fabulous goal on *Match of the Day*. But when the magic was misfiring, his contribution to the team effort was limited.

Ramsey was sometimes pilloried for preferring perspiration to inspiration, but that missed the point. He believed that to make a team work to its maximum, each individual needed to perform on a consistent basis; he was more inclined to favour a player who produced eighty per cent in successive games than one who might reach one hundred per cent in one match but only sixty in the next.

What Ramsey did not realise, or anyone else for that matter, was that Greaves was in fact suffering from the effects of hepatitis. After scoring both goals for Spurs in a league match at the end

of October he was rested and effectively out of action for three months.

Next up for England were Northern Ireland, who were going well in their World Cup group thanks to George Best, who had played in every qualifying match. Up front for England, meanwhile, there were still questions. Peter Osgood had only played a handful of First Division matches for Chelsea, but he was already being touted as the potential answer to England's problems. The player who paid the price was Barry Bridges: Osgood's form had forced him out to the right wing; for England, Bridges found Ramsey preferring the fit-again Peacock. Though Bridges remained in Ramsey's thoughts, his England career was effectively over. His Chelsea career, too, ended when he was sold to Birmingham at the end of the season.

Also back for England for the Northern Ireland match were

RIGHT | November 1965. In a poor match at Wembley, George Best was the best forward on view, here seen tormenting George Cohen and Jack Charlton.

BELOW | Alan Peacock's overhead kick produced the winning goal for England, but this was his last international. Ramsey's search for the right combination up front would continue.

Gordon Banks, Peter Thompson and, for the first time for five years, Arsenal's Joe Baker. Baker had won his first cap in the Winterbottom era – also against Northern Ireland at Wembley – but had later spent a season with Torino in Italy before the Arsenal manager Billy Wright paid £70,000 to bring him to Highbury. Ramsey chose him to partner Peacock, and was rewarded as both men scored in an untidy 2–1 win. Peacock's goal was a clever overhead kick, but his knee was still troubling him, and his season came to an end shortly after Christmas.

For Northern Ireland there was further disappointment. At the end of November, they needed a win to force a play-off against Switzerland, but could only draw their qualifying match in Albania, leaving the Swiss as group winners.

Also failing to qualify were the Republic of Ireland, who in a two-team group following the withdrawal of Syria, lost their play-off against Spain in Paris (Syria, like the other Asian and African nations, had chosen to boycott over the

lack of final places allotted to the two continents; only North Korea remained, who beat Australia home and away to qualify for the last sixteen).

With Wales finishing behind the USSR in their group, that left only Scotland with a chance of qualifying. The Scots had unexpectedly lost at home to Poland, but had regained momentum by beating their main rivals, Italy, at Hampden. To qualify, the Scots needed to win the return match in Naples, with a draw good enough to force a play-off. But Jock Stein's team, much weakened by injuries, were beaten 3–0 and also failed to make the finals.

England's lacklustre performances in the autumn were proof, if proof were needed, of the value of host-nation status. Free of the chores of qualifying, they finally produced a performance which made a mockery of their form in the previous three games – beating Spain, the holders of the European Nations Cup 2–0 in Madrid. The victory has been flagged ever since as the turning point in the campaign to win the World Cup, and as an illustration of Ramsey's tactical genius in discarding wingers altogether in a fluid 4-3-3 formation.

On the morning of 8 December, alongside news of Scotland's defeat in Italy, the *Daily Mail* preview of the England game in the Bernabéu firmly asserted that Ramsey's experiment with Bobby Charlton as the linkman in midfield was over. The newspaper suggested he would return to the left wing, while Alan Ball would replace Peter Thompson on the right.

The report, however, was out of date as soon as the match began, and if anything the Spaniards were even more bewildered. With Stiles patrolling their rear, Eastham and Bobby Charlton were paired in midfield with a brief to break forward on the left as required. Ball's duty was the reverse, starting up front with Baker and Hunt (yet again replacing Greaves!) but tracking back whenever Spain gained possession. The home side's full backs faced the same puzzle posed by Ramsey's Ipswich side: without a conventional winger to mark they could not decide whether to stick or twist.

Following an England free kick, Baker scored the first goal from a Wilson cross, but then limped off, injured. It mattered not.

December 1965. Gordon Banks signs an autograph on his return from England's 2–0 win in Madrid. Many viewed victory against the European champions as a tactical triumph, and a turning point in the campaign to win the World Cup.

Norman Hunter came on for his first cap and fell in alongside his Leeds colleague, Jack Charlton. Bobby Moore moved into midfield and was in an inside right position when his pass was turned in by Hunt. England's mastery was complete, and the Spanish coach José Villalonga admitted that Ramsey's team had been 'superior both in experiment and performance, and could have beaten any team tonight.' *The Times*, meanwhile, was clear that it had witnessed a departure from routine: 'This was football of a new conception. Numbers meant nothing. Every man moved and changed places, bemusing a Spanish side who had clearly set out to play a marking game.'

In an age when television recordings were thin on the ground, the England manager was tempted to keep the 'wingless wonders' tactic under wraps. 'It would be quite wrong to let the rest of the world see exactly what we are doing,' Ramsey told the *Daily Mail*. 'My job is to produce the right team at the right time and that does not always mean pressing on with a certain combination just because it is successful.' With a fine sense of prophecy, the *Mail* added that, in addition to the team in Madrid, 'players like Terry Venables, Johnny Byrne, Martin Peters and Gordon Milne had shown with their clubs that they can accept the new concept.

Others like Greaves and Thompson must still pass this test.'

Like a medieval alchemist, Ramsey had fastened on to a formula for transforming base metal. But, although the final outcome appeared revolutionary, it was part of a process in Ramsey's mind ever since he focused on the fallibility of 4-2-4. In future, to retain one winger might still be possible; two seemed like extravagance.

The truth is that playing without them was not imposed on the England players. It evolved because it suited the particular pattern Ramsey wanted, providing a greater defensive shield while offering more consistent options in attack.

Ever the pragmatist, Ramsey had found – or perhaps stumbled on – the six men who offered freedom from doubt in defence. Ahead of Banks, the back four of Cohen, Jack Charlton, Moore and Wilson was now a given. In front of them, in a change to his club role, was Stiles, the outer moat of England's castle, the ultimate defensive midfielder. He could win enough of the ball, but needed others to process it.

The only other certainty in Ramsey's plan was Bobby Charlton. He was the hub around which attacks could be built, but if Stiles lay deep, an extra player was required – like Eastham in Madrid – to help him provide the necessary creative force. This in turn meant withdrawing a player from the front line, and required those who remained there to work even harder.

The key role, therefore, was that of Alan Ball on the right: he was the one who had the energy both to support the two front men and also to reinforce midfield. The result was that 4-3-3 actually became 4-4-2 when the opposition had the ball, but 4-1-3-2 in attack, with only Stiles minding the store.

Given the result in Spain, it was no surprise that Ramsey intended to select an unchanged team – for the first time since October 1963 – to play against Poland in January. But Bobby Charlton was hurt in a training collision with Tony Waiters, and Gordon Harris of Burnley came in for his first and only cap for England.

The match took place at Goodison Park because a World Cup semi-final was due to be played there – possibly involving England. On a pitch made heavy by rain, the Poles were ahead at half-time after England missed a string of chances. The equaliser came from an unlikely source when George Cohen fought his way down the right and centred for Moore to head in – his first goal for England in his thirty-fifth international.

The following day, 6 January, the draw for the finals took place at the newly built Royal Garden Hotel in London. Of the four groups of four, England's looked less than formidable and the host nation – drawn with Uruguay, Mexico and France – were installed as second favourites behind Brazil. The holders' group included Hungary and Portugal, but it seemed West Germany had a tougher assignment, with Spain and Argentina for company. The virtually unknown North Koreans, meanwhile, would probably have to eliminate either Italy or the Soviet Union to progress to the quarter-finals.

Among the guests at the draw was the vice president of the Italian FA, Dr Ottorino Barassi. During the Second World War, Barassi had hidden the Jules Rimet trophy in a shoebox under his bed to prevent it falling into Fascist hands.

Maybe someone should have asked his advice, because no sooner had Brazil handed the trophy over to the World Cup

RIGHT | Following the draw, England were installed as second favourites behind the holders Brazil. The rank outsiders were North Korea, but they provided the biggest upset of the whole tournament.

Watched by building workers, Bobby Moore and the rest of the England squad limber up at Bellefield ahead of their match against Poland at Goodison Park. The match was staged at Everton's ground because at one point it seemed likely that an England semi-final would be held there. In the end, to the disappointment of many ticket holders, England remained at Wembley.

RIGHT | January 1966. Bobby Moore (out of picture) scores his first goal for England against Poland, played at Goodison Park. The nearest England player is Joe Baker, who had scored in the previous two matches, but was yet another forward who missed out on Ramsey's final squad.

Organisation than – to their utter embarrassment – it was stolen. FIFA had agreed for it to be shown, under close guard, at the Stampex exhibition in Westminster. But on the morning of Sunday 20 March, the fourteen-inch-high trophy was found to be missing. Thankfully, a week later, it was found under a hedge in South London by a man taking his dog for a walk. The black-and-white mongrel, Pickles, owned by Dave Corbett, became an instant celebrity (see pages 170–1).

The World Cup trophy wasn't the only thing hidden from view that spring. A few weeks earlier England played host to West Germany at Wembley on 23 February. Alf Ramsey, unwilling to show his opponents his full hand, decided to make a number of changes. Norman Hunter earned his first full cap, which meant Bobby Moore played further forward. There was a first cap, too, for the Blackburn full back Keith Newton, as the England manager searched for back-up to the pair of Cohen and Wilson. With Greaves only just returning to full fitness, there was yet another change up front. Joe Baker, who one minute seemed to have cemented an England place, now found himself no longer a fixture in his own club side. Both he and George

Eastham had been dropped by Arsenal, and two days after the West Germany game, Baker was transferred to Nottingham Forest.

In his place came Geoff Hurst, son of a former professional and in a rich vein of form for West Ham. Once a journeyman wing half,

ABOVE | Geoff Hurst seems out of step in this squad picture taken before his debut against West Germany. Back row left to right: Cohen, Stiles, Baker, Thompson, Banks, Eastham, Springett, Milne, Flowers, Wilson, Reaney, Greaves, Harris, Hunter, Hunt and Shepherdson (Asst Manager). Front row: Jack Charlton, Newton, Ball, Hurst, Bobby Charlton and Moore.

Hurst had been asked to play up front by manager Ron Greenwood: a move which transformed his career. Hurst could score goals – he would end this season with forty for West Ham in all competitions – but Ramsey had also been impressed by his eagerness to make runs for his colleagues, his willingness to show for a pass and his strength to hold the ball up until reinforcements arrived. If England at times trusted in only two players up front, might not Hurst be one of them?

The first England–West Germany match of 1966 was short on drama and decided by a single goal, again from a Cohen cross.

Hunt's header was only parried by Tilkowski in the German goal and, as it stopped virtually on the goal line, Nobby Stiles – wearing the number nine shirt – scored his first and only goal for his country. Keith Newton's debut finished soon afterwards when he collided with Banks and was replaced by Wilson. By the end there were boos from the crowd for a less-than-impressive England performance. As for the manager, Ramsey again grumbled that chances had not been taken.

Just over a month later, Ramsey's mood was somewhat different as England gave him a first win as manager over Scotland.

Ramsey fielded a 4-3-3 formation at Hampden Park, with John Connelly returning, but *The Times* still pined for the more predictable days of 4-2-4: 'While Scotland will use the flanks, England stick to the plan which simmers in Mr Ramsey's head. For three matches we have been without wingers; now we have only Connelly.'

In fact, with Ball and Charlton dominant in midfield, England were two up in half an hour thanks to Hurst and Hunt. A typical header

by Law from a corner just before half-time gave the 133,000 crowd hope, but Hunt soon restored England's two-goal lead. Jimmy Johnstone on the Scottish right bothered Newton all afternoon and scored either side of a Bobby Charlton strike. To Ramsey's relief, Stiles cleared off the line in the last minute, and the match finished 4–3 in England's favour.

Reports of England's fine display were no match for a major news story the following Monday involving Bobby Moore. As captain of West Ham he had lifted the FA Cup and the Cup Winners' Cup at Wembley in successive seasons, but, according to his manager, Ron Greenwood, his prized defender had been coasting through the current season. There were rumours that Spurs wanted to sign him along with Chelsea captain Terry Venables.

Two days before West Ham faced Borussia Dortmund in the semi-final of the trophy they had won the previous May, Greenwood sacked Moore as captain. He told journalist Brian Scovell, 'Moore has not been really playing for us for eight months … to be a big-time player you have to play like a big-time player every time.'

According to Greenwood, Moore took the news of his demotion 'without a flicker of emotion. I'm not sure he ever did show any.' For Ramsey there were echoes of his stance two years earlier when he delayed naming Moore as captain without being assured of his loyalty to the cause. This new situation would not be solved so easily, but solved it had to be. FA rules said that only registered players could be picked for England, and Moore's contract was due to end on 30 June. Without a contract with West Ham, or any other club, Moore would be out of the World Cup finals.

For the Dortmund match, Greenwood chose Budgie Byrne to lead out West Ham, a decision which must have amused Moore. The new Hammers captain was still a mile away from being a role model: following his injury in an England shirt twelve months earlier, the West Ham staff had toiled to get his knee right, only for Byrne to injure it again when jumping off a stagecoach on their summer tour of the USA. In December Byrne had to be put to bed after drinking heavily on the plane before a cup tie in Greece, but had then played brilliantly on the night to help West Ham through. This time there was a less happy outcome. Moore was booed by fans at Upton Park, and Dortmund, with Tilkowski, Held and Emmerich in their side, won 5–2 on aggregate to secure their place against Liverpool in the final at Hampden Park.

The repercussions of the Moore affair were still felt a month later when England met Yugoslavia on 4 May. The captain was left out and replaced by Hunter. As for the new England captain, Ramsey merely selected the old one. He had not forgotten Jimmy Armfield, even while he was out of the side. 'In March, Alf came to see me play for Blackpool,' Armfield remembers, 'and said that I was back to my best. He told me George Cohen was established at right back, but he wanted me in the World Cup squad as an experienced player who could step in if necessary.' Armfield wasn't the only familiar face returning: with Hunt preparing to play for Liverpool against Dortmund the next day, Greaves was once more selected, having been out of the side since the defeat by Austria.

The main talking point, however, was the award of a first cap for the elegant West Ham midfielder, Martin Peters. As a boy Peters had excelled at all sports, but was always likely to end up as a footballer. As Ron Greenwood recalled, 'It would be ridiculous to say anyone discovered him. He was public knowledge.' As a fifteen-year-old Peters had played at Wembley, in front of a 95,000 crowd, for England Schoolboys against West Germany, whose team that day included Wolfgang Overath. The two men would oppose each other again several times, not least in the 1966 World Cup final.

Peters was so talented that, having signed for West Ham, Greenwood's only problem was which position suited him best.

RIGHT | Nobby Stiles, Billy Bremner (in an England shirt) and Alan Ball leave the field after the match. For the second match in succession, the combination of Hurst and Hunt up front gave Ramsey food for thought.

Some thought he lacked steel, and he was dropped at one stage, missing West Ham's FA Cup final win in 1964. But Peters was no soft touch, and now, two years on, he was a regular for West Ham and back at Wembley for his first full international.

Replacing Stiles for the match again Yugoslavia, Peters looked comfortable throughout, complementing Bobby Charlton in midfield and getting forward to support Hurst and Greaves up front. Greaves headed England ahead with his thirty-ninth goal for his country. Bobby Charlton, recently named Footballer of the Year, thumped in the second from twenty-five yards via the crossbar: his thirty-seventh international goal. Even so, Ramsey again complained afterwards that England should have scored more.

Two days after the Yugoslavia match Ramsey announced the twenty-eight players who would attend the World Cup training

camp at Lilleshall on 6 June. Three of them came from outside the forty players he had originally chosen in April – well ahead of the FIFA deadline (see page 252). Marvin Hinton and Barry Bridges were replaced by Brian Labone and Bobby Tambling, while Fred Pickering gave way to the irrepressible Budgie Byrne. For Pickering, there was further disappointment a week later when he was replaced in Everton's FA Cup final team by the relatively unknown Mike Trebilcock, who scored twice in the defeat of Sheffield Wednesday.

Others left out of the twenty-eight included Tony Waiters, with Ron Springett and the uncapped Peter Bonetti preferred. Ramsey also chose to ignore the press clamour for Peter Osgood, whose time would come later. Terry Venables was another casualty: having fallen out again with Tommy Docherty, he'd been transferred to Spurs in time to play in their last league match of the season, but would never add to the two caps awarded by Ramsey.

The squad included eleven players from the twenty-two selected for Chile four years earlier. Even with Chris Lawler and Tommy Smith left out, there were still five Liverpool players remaining, including the uncapped Ian Callaghan. This was not surprising: Liverpool had comfortably won the league and only lost in the Cup Winners' Cup final in the very last minute. Terry Paine's Southampton had just been promoted, which meant there was only one player from the Second Division, Ron Flowers of Wolves. For all of them, the hard work was about to begin.

'FOR ALL OF THEM, THE HARD WORK WAS ABOUT TO BEGIN'

LEFT | May 1966. Jimmy Greaves (white shirt, centre of picture) returns for England and scores the first goal in the 2–0 win against Yugoslavia. Two days later Ramsey announced the twenty-eight players to attend the World Cup training camp at Lilleshall.

June 1966. The England squad
pose in front of the main house at
Lilleshall, in Shropshire. The players
had enjoyed a short break at the end
of the domestic season, but now faced
days of competitive and intensive
training after which Alf Ramsey would
announce his final squad of twenty-two
for the finals, beginning on 11 July.

PICKLES...

BEFORE ENGLAND won the World Cup in 1966, they lost it. For a week the theft captured the attention of the nation. The trophy, originally called Victory, had been renamed the Jules Rimet Trophy in 1946 in honour of the FIFA president who had pushed through the idea of a World Cup in the first place. Including the base, the gold-plated sterling silver trophy stood fourteen inches high.

After being handed over to the World Cup Organisation at the draw in January 1966, it was agreed that the trophy – insured for £30,000 – could be displayed at the Stampex Exhibition taking place in the Central Hall, Westminster. It was taken there on 18 March, but 48 hours later – on the morning of Sunday 20 March, when the exhibition was not open – the cabinet was found broken and the trophy gone.

Later that week the chairman of the Football Association, Joe Mears, received a phone call from a man demanding money for its safe return. A detachable part of the trophy was also sent to Mears' house. On Friday 25 March, police arranged a rendezvous with, and later arrested, a man in connection with the theft. His name was Edward Bletchley, a petty criminal who denied stealing the trophy but was later convicted of 'demanding money with menaces, with intent to steal'.

Two days later, on 27 March, Dave Corbett was walking his dog Pickles near his home in Beulah Hill in south-east London. The black-and-white mongrel found a small statue wrapped in newspaper under a hedge. Corbett instantly realised he had found the trophy: 'When I tore the paper away I saw the names of Uruguay, Germany and Brazil, and being a football fan I knew it had been stolen.'

Corbett collected a £3,000 reward, but his dog became an instant celebrity. Pickles won a year's supply of dog food, and was later introduced to the crowds outside the Royal Kensington Hotel after England's victory. He even appeared in a spoof feature film with Laurence Harvey, Lionel Jeffries and Eric Sykes called The Spy with a Cold Nose.

The trophy which Bobby Moore raised high on 30 July was next received by Brazil in 1970, who were allowed to keep it, having won it for a third time. A new trophy, the current FIFA

World Cup, was first presented to West Germany, the winners in 1974. Sadly, the Jules Rimet trophy was stolen again, from the Brazilian Football Federation's offices in 1983. But by then Pickles had passed away, and the famous old trophy has never been found.

MARTIN PETERS

OF THE three West Ham players who won the 1966 World Cup, Martin Peters always seemed to be the third man, in the shadow of his two club colleagues. Even though he scored what might have proved the winning goal in the final, Hurst's hat-trick and Moore's captaincy gave them a greater profile in the eyes of the public.

Yet Peters was arguably a more talented footballer than either of them. And though sometimes criticised for being too easy-going, he was the first of the three to leave the East End club.

Born at Plaistow in November 1943, it was soon obvious to all that Peters had a gift for games. At school he was head boy, but the only question, given his mastery of both football and cricket, was which professional sport he would pursue. In the end football won, and after winning six caps for England Schoolboys, and being sought after by every club in London, he signed for West Ham. His manager Ron Greenwood recalled that 'He was tall, lithe and well balanced, and never in a hurry. He did everything so perfectly he made it look too easy.'

Peters made his debut for West Ham at Easter 1962, replacing Geoff Hurst at right half, but could play anywhere. In only his third match for the club he took over as an emergency goalkeeper against Cardiff. Later in his career Alf Ramsey famously called him 'a player ten years ahead of this time', meaning that Peters' versatility should be highly valued. He is probably the only English player who would have fitted into the Dutch teams of the 1970s.

Youth and under-23 caps followed, but at Christmas 1963 his seemingly pre-ordained path to an England cap hit a bump in the road. At Upton Park on Boxing Day, Peters was part of a West Ham side dismantled by Blackburn Rovers, whose 8–2 win included a hat-trick for Fred Pickering.

Two days later, with Peters replaced by the more physical Eddie Bovington, the Hammers won 3–1 at Ewood Park, and then began a run which would end in an FA Cup final win against Preston. Peters watched from the stands at Wembley that day, and never played in an FA Cup final.

But the young man could not be kept out for long. A year later he was in the team that won the Cup Winners' Cup, and in May 1966 Ramsey chose him for his first England cap. Peters said later he'd heard rumours of his selection from a friend with a contact at the official programme printers. Whatever the case, he was the final piece of Ramsey's jigsaw – the last of the eleven who won the World Cup final to play a full international.

Earlier, on his twenty-first birthday, Peters married his girlfriend, Kathy, and the couple moved into a semi-detached house in Hornchurch. In the other half of the house were Geoff and Judith Hurst. The four of them were good friends and would often have nights out together. Peters, however, was never much of a drinker and typically, after the World Cup final banquet, with England players partying all over London, he and his wife stayed behind in the hotel.

His international career began in triumph, but the years that followed proved disappointing. Four years later Peters scored England's second goal in the quarter-final in León, only for West Germany to win in extra time. Then, in 1973, he was captain of the side that could only manage a draw against Poland at Wembley, putting England out of the World Cup.

By that time Peters was a Spurs player. In 1970, he became the first domestic £200,000 footballer in a deal which took Jimmy Greaves to West Ham.

Peters had become increasingly aware that to win further trophies he would have to leave Upton Park. The club were struggling in the league and Greenwood had actually left him out of the side for four games. In his autobiography, Peters recalls the time when he first talked to Tottenham: 'There was no haggling on my part. I wasn't leaving West Ham for more money. Our negotiations took about an hour. I was sorry to be leaving my friends. Not just Bobby and Geoff but all of them. But I wanted to experience more success at club level and doubted whether I could do that at West Ham. As it turned out they didn't win another trophy until 1975.'

At Spurs, Peters enjoyed League Cup and European success, and finished his career with Norwich, and then as player manager of Sheffield United. Like so many of the 1966 team, he found management neither easy nor enjoyable, and he was sacked after United were relegated in 1981.

A few years earlier, Peters had been shocked to hear of Alf Ramsey's sacking by the FA. The two had become close, and Peters, while working in the motor-insurance business, often called in for a cup of tea when he was in the area: 'We'd both lived and gone to school in Dagenham, and both played for Spurs. I continued seeing him for years, still in the same semi-detached house. I always felt his departure could have been handled in a more gentlemanly fashion. There was no reason to treat him so shabbily.'

Sometimes he would call and find Ramsey was out – on the golf course or elsewhere. 'In that case,' said Peters, decent and loyal to the end, 'I'll just drive over there, and wait for him.'

9: TERMINATION

JUNE 1966

ABOVE | Alf Ramsey is suitably unamused by the TV crews wanting pictures of the England World Cup squad at Lilleshall.

DEEP IN THE HEART OF THE SHROPSHIRE COUNTRYSIDE LIES LILLESHALL HALL, BUILT IN 1831 AS A HUNTING LODGE FOR THE DUKE OF SUTHERLAND.

After the Second World War its impressive grounds were purchased by the Central Council of Physical Recreation as a national centre for sport, to complement Bisham Abbey in the south of England.

It was here that in June 1966 Ramsey brought twenty-seven players – one less than anticipated after Brian Labone dropped out. The Everton defender, who had not played for England since Ramsey's first match, was always likely to be reserve to Jack Charlton, and in any case had planned his wedding for the close season. He would be first choice four years later in Mexico. The players had enjoyed a short rest after the season ended, but now training began in earnest. The Lilleshall experience was short on luxury: players were divided four or five to a dormitory, and served and cleared away their own meals.

Ramsey was assisted by his loyal number two, Harold Shepherdson, Les Cocker from Leeds United and Wilf McGuinness from Manchester United, who each supervised a small group of players for a time and then passed them on to the next trainer.

A typical day began with breakfast and a tough physical session, an afternoon of other sports like tennis – Greaves and Eastham were the doubles pair to beat – before dinner and a film. Bedtime was at ten o'clock, whether the film had finished or not!

Knowing what was at stake, and the fact that five of them – after all their hard work – would be obliged to miss the World Cup finals, the sessions were never less than competitive.

ABOVE | Brian Labone and fiancée Patricia Lynam. The Everton captain withdrew from Ramsey's squad because he was getting married in the close season.

The England squad at Lilleshall. Back row (L to R): Greaves, Eastham, Callaghan, Hurst, Hunter, Thompson, Gerry Byrne, Hunt, Bobby Charlton, Connelly, Milne, Springett, Armfield, Moore. Front row: Banks, Bonetti (hidden), Flowers, Cohen, Jack Charlton, Peters, Johnny Byrne, Newton, Paine, Ball and Stiles. Wilson and Tambling are missing from the line up.

George Cohen had been in hospital with a leg injury after the league season ended. Now he was worked like never before by Les Cocker to ensure he would answer every call. Jack Charlton and Nobby Stiles came to blows in a practice match, despite the fact there was nearly eight inches in height between them. Alan Ball lay awake at night, 'telling myself I was doing fine, but that tomorrow I had to be even better. If there were to be any races, any challenges, nobody would beat me. I had to stay in that squad whatever it took.'

Jack Charlton occasionally walked the mile or so to the front gate, putting his arm through the bars and shouting to passing cars to let him out. However, it was Ball and Stiles who figured in one of the few real bids for freedom. One evening, joined by John Connelly, they sneaked off to the nearby golf clubhouse for a beer. Fear of being found out made their stay a swift one, but on their return McGuinness told them Ramsey was looking for them. When confronted, Ball and Stiles offered abject apologies to the England

manager, only for the outspoken Connelly to challenge the manager: 'We only had one pint, which isn't going to do us any harm after the training we've been doing.' Stiles still shudders at what might have happened to them: 'We could have been sent home. But in the end Ramsey, with a face like thunder, just told us all to get out of his sight.' That was enough for Stiles: he was too nervous later to ask Ramsey for a few hours' leave to attend the birth of his second child.

It was in these claustrophobic days that the club atmosphere to which Ramsey had always aspired was built up. No cliques were allowed to blossom; Ramsey, too, was careful in practice matches to mix up the bibs so that there was no recognised first team or reserves.

Understandably, however, there was speculation. 'Obviously I knew the other Liverpool lads,' recalled Gordon Milne, 'and between us we tried to pick the team – who was going to make the twenty-two and who wasn't. It was a pretty intense time.

I remember Ian Callaghan and Roger Hunt saying this was just not going to happen for them. Funnily enough, when we went through the names, we never reckoned there had to be three keepers.'

On the last day at Lilleshall, the decision was made as to who made the final squad. Milne was one of the unlucky ones: 'There were some big rooms at Lilleshall. Alf was sitting on a sofa in one of them and called me in. He said how difficult it was to leave anybody out, thanked me for all my hard work, and that was it. Even then I didn't know the whole story. I only learned the entire squad from listening to the car radio. Looking back now, I might not have been at my best, but I was very surprised Peter Thompson didn't make it.'

Milne was unfortunate. The late arrival on the scene of the adaptable Peters, a proven goalscorer for West Ham, had given Ramsey a further option in midfield. Milne's colleague Thompson had seemed a certainty at one stage, but proved to be less versatile than the three wingers who remained. Tellingly, in eight matches so far for England, Thompson had yet to score a single goal.

One player who only just made the cut was Ray Wilson. Earlier in the fortnight Wilson had ricked his back so badly that his roommate Bobby Charlton had to help him shave. It took a few punishing days

ABOVE | Jimmy Greaves, here signing for a young fan, was not the best of trainers, but on the England tour of Scandinavia, 'never worked harder in his life'.

with Les Cocker before Ramsey was convinced that Wilson could be risked. In reserve, his choice of Liverpool's iron man Gerry Byrne was something of a surprise: Byrne's only international appearance was the Scotland match in 1963, and he had earlier booked a holiday in Majorca, such were his expectations. His inclusion meant the end of the road – for now at least – for Keith Newton.

Two forwards had to pruned. Bobby Tambling, who had played in both Ramsey's first match as manager and the most recent one, was one casualty; Budgie Byrne was the other. In the last three years, Ramsey's choice of centre forwards had come and gone: Smith was too old; Jones too green; Peacock, Pickering and Wignall were held back by injury; Bridges and Baker, discarded by their clubs.

For much of this time, the ebullient Byrne had offered Ramsey a different option. Now he too was dismissed, but not without a typical parting line. The England players, in one of the rare examples of team sponsorship, had each been issued with rainwear by a company called Barracuda. On learning of his rejection, Byrne said, 'OK, Alf, understood. But can we keep the coats?'

The unlucky five of Byrne, Tambling, Newton, Milne and Thompson were asked to stay in training, given that the final deadline for team squads was not until 2 July. The others were sent home for a few days before the tour of Scandinavia and Poland. On the coaching side, there was no room on the tour either for McGuinness: 'Alf told me the FA were being very tight and would not pay for me to go with the others. But he said when we win the World Cup – and it was when not if – you'll be celebrating with us afterwards. And sure enough, at the banquet that night, he found a place for me at his table. A tremendous man.'

In addition to slimming down the squad, Ramsey also issued the shirt numbers. Here he seemed – certainly in the players' minds – to have shown his hand with regard to his first-choice eleven:

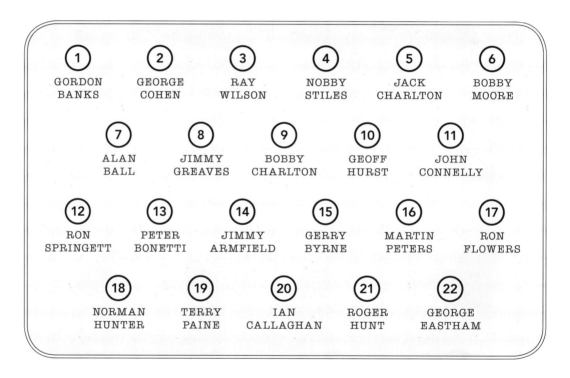

① GORDON BANKS
② GEORGE COHEN
③ RAY WILSON
④ NOBBY STILES
⑤ JACK CHARLTON
⑥ BOBBY MOORE
⑦ ALAN BALL
⑧ JIMMY GREAVES
⑨ BOBBY CHARLTON
⑩ GEOFF HURST
⑪ JOHN CONNELLY
⑫ RON SPRINGETT
⑬ PETER BONETTI
⑭ JIMMY ARMFIELD
⑮ GERRY BYRNE
⑯ MARTIN PETERS
⑰ RON FLOWERS
⑱ NORMAN HUNTER
⑲ TERRY PAINE
⑳ IAN CALLAGHAN
㉑ ROGER HUNT
㉒ GEORGE EASTHAM

'When he read out the numbers I was worried at first,' said Roger Hunt. 'But I was determined not to let it show. You knew Alf wanted players he could depend on, who would give one hundred per cent every time, and so my attitude was: if you're in the squad, keep going, and your chance will come.' He was spot on: when England

played their first match of the 1966 World Cup finals, the only change from the one to eleven shirts above was that Hunt himself replaced Hurst.

With four internationals in ten days, Ramsey ensured that all twenty-two players started at least one game and would enter the finals match-fit. In Finland on 26 June, he retained Hunter as well as Armfield as captain, paired Hunt and Hurst up front and gave Ian Callaghan his first cap on the wing.

The flexible role assigned to Peters was highlighted by the TV commentary for England's first goal: 'Hurst is down the left, and there's Peters in the middle – where you'd expect a centre forward to be – and he's scored!' Ball missed a penalty, but Hunt added a second from a Callaghan cross and Jack Charlton was credited with England's third. The only minus point was that Armfield injured a toe near the end and would be unavailable for the next match in Oslo.

Ramsey made nine changes for the match against Norway, including the return of Moore and Greaves, the latter scoring four

ABOVE | The twelve days of hard work at Lilleshall helped develop a true club atmosphere among the players. There were no cliques and no recognisable first team and reserves. At the end, however, five players heard the news that they were out of Ramsey's twenty-two-man squad.

goals in England's 6–1 victory. The BBC's reporter Frank Bough, accompanying the tour, was impressed: 'For so long weakened by his illness, in Oslo the little genius re-announced himself. With a natural inclination to idleness, Greaves has never trained harder in his life. Not that any of them have had much choice. Punishment until it hurts is Ramsey's method.'

The following day, the squad had some rare time off, playing golf and sightseeing while the manager went to watch Brazil play Sweden in Gothenburg. Ramsey returned with surprising news: Brazil had won 3–2, but their ageing defence, he assured his players, would prevent the champions of 1958 and 1962 progressing far in 1966.

For the third tour match against Denmark, Ramsey gave Peter Bonetti the first of his seven England caps. The last one, of course, came four years later in Mexico, when he replaced Banks at the last minute and was widely blamed for England's defeat by West Germany. Here in Copenhagen he was rarely troubled, as England won 2–0 thanks to a fine header by Jack Charlton and a rare goal

from George Eastham. Up front, Hurst was paired with Greaves, who was playing his fiftieth international: but on a poor pitch the West Ham player, as he admitted later, really struggled to find his best form.

As a result, Hurst was left out of the final tour match on 5 July against Poland in Katowice – a venue reached by Ramsey and his squad after a tedious journey involving two flights and a long coach ride. So far, the manager had used at least one winger in his preferred 4-3-3 formation, but now he reverted to his 'Madrid' version of 4-1-3-2, with Ball and Peters alongside Bobby Charlton, and only Hunt and Greaves as recognised front players. The usual defensive line-up repelled all that the Poles could throw at them, and Hunt scored the only goal of the match with a brilliant strike from long range. In all, the four games had produced twelve goals with only one conceded, and thankfully no injuries. The next day the players were up at dawn for the return to England. They would be allowed a short time at home, before assembling again in London at the weekend.

On the eve of the tournament, Ramsey was asked by BBC Television to assess his time in charge. In his somewhat stilted style, he told them, 'When news of my appointment, that is my appointment as England team manger, was made, and when surrounded by all and sundry, that is the press, TV, and radio, the obvious question was asked of me, how will "England get on?" Without any consideration I said that England would win the World Cup competition.

'After two defeats (to begin with), for the next match against Brazil, the players would now be disciplined to a set pattern whereby each player knew what was expected of them.

For two years we persevered with a 4-2-4 system, which enabled us to make up some of the lost ground, and most certainly was satisfactory result-wise with regard to matches played in this country. In 1964 we lost our way a little in South America. Although the players played as well as they could, bearing in mind that England players are never at their best following a strenuous season, the margin of difference was in finishing ability where we fell well below the South

American teams. In the last two years, we have improved to some extent. If players have had indifferent matches they have been persevered with, particularly those you feel confident have more ability than they have shown in a particular match. During this time a good number of players have been tried, and we have finally reached the players that will represent England. I am not suggesting for one moment that they are the best twenty-two players in the country, but most certainly they are twenty-two of the best players in the country. The late start to the competition has helped and England I'm certain will do well. I also think it will take a really great side to beat England.'

For Ramsey there was one final piece of unfinished business. On his arrival at Hendon Hall – the team's headquarters for the tournament – he summoned Ron Greenwood to the hotel and stuck him in a room with Bobby Moore. The England captain's contract with West Ham had lapsed on 30 June and, without a new one, Moore was technically ineligible to play international football. There was little discussion between the two men. Moore signed a temporary deal to expire the day after the World Cup final. If England made it that far, he would at least be allowed to play.

NOBBY STILES

THE SIGHT of Nobby Stiles, all five feet six inches of him and front teeth missing, doing a jig of delight with the trophy in his hands, is one of the iconic images of England's World Cup victory.

Here was the ultimate triumph of the little man and proof, if proof were needed, that it takes all types to make a successful football team. Stiles, wearing number four for England, was never going to match the elegance of the West German wearing the same number: Franz Beckenbauer. But his role in the England set-up was just as significant. 'My job,' said Stiles, 'was to win the ball, and give it to Bobby Charlton.'

That modest statement hides a life's work of reducing famous forwards, including the likes of Eusebio, to tears. Being marked by Stiles – whose position today would be called the holding midfielder – was like being pursued by a rather annoying dog. He could bite you if necessary, but mostly he made your life a misery by following you around, pinching your ball and running off with it.

Stiles was born into a strict Catholic family, during a German air raid close to his home in Manchester in May 1942. In some ways his career matched the spirit of those days: working together to overcome adversity, to first survive and then move on.

As a boy, Stiles was taught by John Mulligan at St Patrick's in Collyhurst, a school with a famous footballing tradition. In his autobiography *After the Ball*, he recalled the lesson he received after trying to impress in a trial for Manchester Boys: 'I'd scored a goal but he told me I had played poorly because I hadn't played for the team. I learned that football was something you could not just take as you liked, how it suited you. You had to understand how you fitted into the team and what your best contribution could be.'

Stiles was good enough to play five times for England Schoolboys, and was an apprentice with Manchester United at the time of the Munich air crash in which his hero Eddie Colman died. After making his league debut in midfield in 1960, Stiles was in and out of the first team, but found an unlikely champion in goalkeeper Harry Gregg. It was Gregg who realised that Stiles, for all his positional awareness, was actually struggling to see the ball properly.

Once Stiles was issued with big, hard contact lenses, and a special fluid to prevent dryness, his career flourished.

Gregg's praise for Stiles is absolute: 'As a young man at Old Trafford he had to fight for every chance he got. I remember early on someone saying he was just a good utility player, but I told him Stiles was the best wing half in the club. Quite honestly there were times when he should have drawn the wages of some of those he played with. He not only did his job; he made sure everyone else did theirs.'

Norman Hunter of Leeds, no weakling himself, also realised the value of Stiles to both club and country: 'A lovely man off the field. An absolute gent. But when he took those teeth out he became a different person. I'm telling you, on the field you did not cross Nobby at all.'

There were many who scoffed when Stiles was picked for England against Scotland in 1965. By then for his club he had dropped into a back four role alongside the centre half. Ramsey, though, wanted him to play a different role, as a 'screen' in front of fellow debutant Jack Charlton and Bobby Moore.

The match was the making of Stiles as an England player. Because of injuries, the team was reduced in the second half to nine fit men, and he was at the heart of a resistance effort which ended in a 2–2 draw. From that day on, Ramsey's half back line of choice read Stiles, Charlton, Moore.

In the 1966 finals there was a moment of controversy when his badly timed tackle injured the French forward Jacky Simon. Ramsey was pressured by FIFA to leave Stiles out of the next match, but his reply was unambiguous: 'If I am forced to replace him, you will be looking for another manager'. In the next niggling match Stiles kept a close eye on the clever Argentinian, Onega, and in the semi-final produced probably his finest effort in an England shirt, shadowing the dangerous Eusebio. Late in the game Jack Charlton's handball allowed the Portuguese star to score from a penalty, but there was still time for Stiles to

somehow prevent Simões scoring, which would have meant extra time.

In the dressing room afterwards Ramsey was clear that Stiles' contribution had been crucial: 'I rarely talk about individuals, but I think you will all agree that Nobby has today turned in a very professional performance.'

For a player with such a sense of timing, Stiles was a basket case away from football. Everything from cars to cameras refused to work for him. Bobby Charlton called him 'Clouseau', after the hapless policeman made famous by Peter Sellers, and in his autobiography recalled a typical morning in the life of Stiles:

'Nobby and I were sharing a room at Euston after an England match. When we woke up we had about an hour to catch the train. When Nobby drew the curtains he managed to pull them onto the floor. He tried to switch off the radio and it fell off the wall. Finally he collided with the glass shelf with our shaving gear on it and the whole thing crashed down.'

The two friends and colleagues figured in a famous night two years after winning the World Cup: Stiles again nullifying Eusebio as Manchester United beat Benfica to win the European Cup. But by then he was feeling the effect of knee injuries, and his place in the England team had been taken by Alan Mullery. His last international was against Scotland in 1970, after which Stiles made Ramsey's squad in Mexico but was not called upon to play.

The following year he joined Middlesbrough, and then finished his playing career with Preston, led briefly by his old pal Bobby Charlton. Stiles later managed the club himself for a time, and was assistant to his brother-in-law Johnny Giles at West Brom. Nobby is married to Giles' sister, and they have three boys, the eldest of which, John Stiles, played for Leeds and Doncaster Rovers.

There have been some tough times for Stiles since he finished playing, and his health – after suffering a heart attack in 2002 – is not good. But all who played with him remember him with love and affection. For George Cohen, however, affection once went too far. When the final whistle blew at Wembley in 1966, Stiles jumped on him and gave him a big, toothless kiss. 'It was,' Cohen is reported to have said, 'the nearest thing to copulation. And in front of the Queen as well.'

10: EXPECTATION

JULY 1966

July 1966. Groups of boys representing each of the sixteen competing nations practise their line-up for the Opening Ceremony. The early rehearsals were a shambles until a regimental sergeant major lent a hand to proceedings.

THE FIRST REHEARSAL FOR THE OPENING CEREMONY WAS A SHAMBLES. THE SECOND WAS NOT MUCH BETTER.

The teams of boy scouts representing the sixteen competing nations were supposed to exit from the players' tunnel to the sound of the massed bands of the Brigade of Guards. However, as they entered the stadium, the groups were either too far apart or so bunched up that one 'country' collided with the back of another.

In the TV truck which would transmit the start of the 1966 finals, producer Alec Weeks was in despair. There was not much time before the real thing would be shown around the world. 'The FA officials had all given up,' he recalled, 'but suddenly there appeared the biggest regimental sergeant major the Guards have ever produced, who set to work with the scouts. Afternoon turned into evening, and the next day we started all over again. There were tears and sore feet, but somehow a shamble became a saunter, the saunter a walk, the walk a march. And in the end the lads did the Guards proud.'

Like the scouts at the first rehearsal, the public also seemed out of step with the event. Despite the World Cup Willie campaign and the cheapness of tournament tickets, England's opening match against Uruguay on Monday 11 July was a few thousand short of a sell-out: something unthinkable today.

Alf Ramsey had made up his mind quite early about how he wanted to play against the South Americans. The only change from the previous match in Poland was to replace Martin Peters with a winger in John Connelly, on the assumption that England were likely to have the lion's share of possession. True to form, the

LEFT | 11 July. England supporters – most in collar and tie – make their way to Wembley Stadium for the opening game. Surprisingly, tickets were still available on the day for the match with Uruguay.

South Americans packed their defence and offered little threat: the corner kick count at the end of the match was 16–1 in favour of the home side. Connelly hit the post, and Hunt and Greaves roamed endlessly, but the result – not for the last time in opening World Cup matches – was a goalless draw.

The *Daily Mail* called the result more of a blow to prestige than to the prospects of winning the World Cup, but foreign correspondents were not so accommodating. The Swedish paper *Dagens Nyheter* suggested that, 'The goalkeepers had a holiday. No one wants to pay to see eight defenders crawl around their penalty area like Uruguay. It seems the football will be as boring as it was in Chile.'

In France, *L'Équipe* was in confident mood: 'England lacked class and Uruguay lacked ambition. France could not lose to this England team, and will beat Uruguay.' As it happens, it was wrong on both counts.

Ramsey responded by taking the squad to relax at Pinewood Studios, where they mingled with the likes of Yul Brynner, Norman Wisdom and Sean Connery. At one point the players crept quietly on to the set to watch filming of the latest James Bond film, only for the scene to need restaging when Ray Wilson, after one beer too many, fell off his chair. In his speech of thanks at the end of the afternoon, Ramsey pronounced Connery's Christian name 'Seen' – a gaffe made more prominent by the giggles emanating from Greaves and Moore.

For the second group match against Mexico on 16 July, Ramsey replaced Connelly with another winger, Terry Paine, and brought in Peters for Alan Ball. The latter was incensed for a short time and talked about leaving the squad, but was persuaded otherwise by Jimmy Greaves.

The match was drifting away from England until towards half-time, when Bobby Charlton received the ball in his own half, ran forward virtually unchallenged and hit a right-foot shot past Calderon from more than twenty-five yards. The Mexican goalkeeper never got a hand to it. He did, however, push away a Greaves shot in the second half, only for the ball to fall kindly for

RIGHT | Three and half years after taking the job, the England manager Alf Ramsey leads out his team for the opening match of the 1966 World Cup finals, which finished in a dull 0–0 draw.

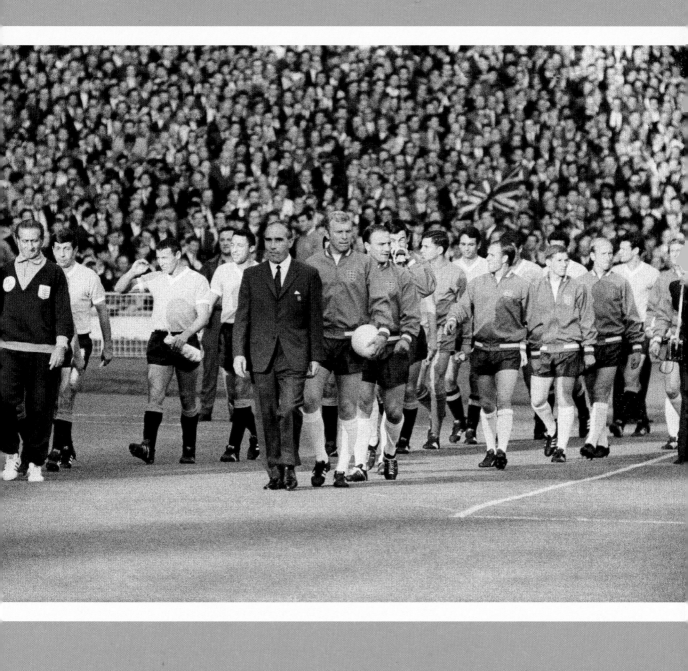

Hunt, to make the score 2–0. In the dressing room later, all agreed that Hunt's running off the ball had played a big part in Charlton's superb goal.

So far the games in England's group had failed to resonate, but elsewhere there were signs that the competition was starting to catch fire. At Goodison Park, the holders and favourites, Brazil, minus the injured Pelé, had been beaten by Hungary in a thrilling match. West Germany had unveiled the elegant Franz Beckenbauer in cruising past Switzerland and then showed steel in the draw with Argentina, who had Jorge Albrecht sent off. At Ayresome Park, the North Koreans had started with a defeat and a draw and would now take on Italy.

ABOVE | The day after the Uruguay match the England players paid a visit to Pinewood studios. Ron Springett with Jimmy Greaves and Sean Connery.

England's final group match was against France on 20 July and was again a pedestrian affair. Ramsey's team could manage only two goals, both scored by Hunt: the first was a tap in after Jack Charlton's header had hit a post and rolled along the goal line; the second came from a cross from Ian Callaghan, given his chance on the right wing in place of Paine. Hunt's header was accurate but far from decisive until Aubour in the French goal managed to manipulate the ball over the line.

'I had no idea the pressure would be so severe,' Ramsey said afterwards. 'It has even affected me. Now we have qualified the team will play with much more freedom.'

The post-mortems, however, were mainly about two tackles. The first, by Joseph Bonnel on Jimmy Greaves, was bad enough: playing without pads, it cut through Greaves' shin and required stitches. The second was by an already-booked Nobby Stiles on Jacky Simon. The tackle was late and left the French midfielder in agony on the ground. The incident was reviewed by FIFA, who in turn put pressure on the FA to discipline the player. Ramsey was summoned

BELOW | Training finished, Bobby Charlton (left) shows his hand to the camera but away from Peter Bonetti, Martin Peters, his brother Jack, and Bobby Moore. Meanwhile (right), John Connelly, Roger Hunt and Gerry Byrne work on their tans.

ABOVE | 16 July. The turning point for England. The Mexican goalkeeper, Calderon, leaps in vain to prevent a twenty-five-yard shot from Bobby Charlton entering the net. After a poor start, Ramsey's team were off and running.

to Lancaster Gate by the international committee, who had a mind to demand Stiles be dropped – for one match at least. Ramsey's stance was simple. If he was obliged to leave out Stiles, they would be looking for a new manager, with immediate effect.

Stiles and Ramsey both had key roles to play in the quarter-final against Argentina at Wembley. So too did Alan Ball, still smarting after being dropped for the Mexico match. Ramsey had not seen the South Americans in person before the match, but had watched their games on television at England's HQ and knew where the dangers lay. He told Ball to prevent Marzolini, Argentina's left back, causing problems. Ball told him he would die trying.

The other change to the line-up was to prove more significant. The injury to Greaves was going to take some time to heal and so Geoff Hurst, the only other front player in the squad, replaced him. Now that the tournament had reached the knock-out stage, Ramsey reverted to the 4-1-3-2 format, which banished risk: Stiles would stifle the Argentine playmaker Onega, while Peters and Ball would tuck in alongside Bobby Charlton. All three wingers had had their say. Now Hurst and Hunt would labour alone up front.

There was talk of England's match, live on TV, being moved to the evening to protect attendances at the other games, but FIFA confirmed that all quarter-finals would start at 3 p.m. on 23 July.

In addition to the Wembley match, the line-up for the last eight

'IF HE WAS OBLIGED TO LEAVE OUT STILES, THEY WOULD BE LOOKING FOR A NEW MANAGER, WITH IMMEDIATE EFFECT'

RIGHT | A star is born. Franz Beckenbauer announced himself with two goals as West Germany thrashed Switzerland 5–0 in their opening match.

included Hungary against the USSR, and West Germany against Uruguay. Meanwhile, at Goodison Park, the North Koreans – who had beaten and eliminated Italy in one of the biggest World Cup upsets of all time – faced Portugal, conquerors of Brazil, and the new favourites to win the competition. Pelé, only half fit and the subject of fierce attention from the Portuguese defenders, had limped out of the 1966 World Cup with a towel wrapped round his shoulders. It would be another four years before he returned – in triumph – to the World Cup finals.

The effects of England's match with Argentina are still being felt

today. The South Americans were determined from the start to upset their opponents with a litany of fouls, both seen and unseen by the referee Rudolf Kreitlein of West Germany. Jack Charlton said it was the most boring match he had ever played in, since it was constantly being halted for free kicks.

George Cohen recalled in his autobiography that 'they made everything difficult, arguing, pulling your hair, and making late tackles. At the heart of all the mischief was their captain Rattin, who literally spat out his disgust if decisions didn't go his way.'

It was actually the third time that an England team had faced Antonio Ubaldo Rattin. The Boca Juniors star had played in the Argentine team beaten 3–1 by England four years earlier in Chile and then in the 'Little World Cup' in 1964. His favourite position was in front of the back four, but, in addition to the role performed by Nobby Stiles for England, he was also granted the freedom to go forward and use his immense power to launch attacks.

At six feet four inches, Rattin towered over Kreitlein, constantly disputing his decisions. In the thirty-fifth minute came the explosion. Rattin had already been booked for tripping Bobby Charlton, and, after Artime had also had his name taken, the

ABOVE | 23 July. The winning goal against Argentina, forged on West Ham's training ground.
(Top) Martin Peters on the far touchline has crossed for the unmarked Geoff Hurst to head the ball from
inside the six-yard box (bottom) The beaten goalkeeper, Roma, and colleagues appeal for offside, but
the timing of Hurst's run was perfect.

Argentine captain continued to protest, pointing at his captain's armband. 'Kreitlein reported that he had received a more sinister message from Rattin's words and looks,' wrote Hugh McIlvanney in *The Observer*. 'At any rate, apparently deciding that Rattin was becoming an obstruction to the entire game, the referee ordered him from the field.'

Drama was followed by farce as Rattin refused to leave the pitch. Still arguing, he lingered on the touchline. At one stage it seemed the whole Argentine team would join him, and the match would be abandoned. The FIFA observer Ken Aston, who had refereed the infamous Chile v Italy World Cup match four years earlier, attempted to restore order, and eventually Rattin was persuaded to make his way to the dressing room.

Even with ten men, and in a heatwave, Argentina remained a threat. Until, that is, a move manufactured on West Ham's training ground broke the deadlock. Martin Peters drifted out to the left wing and, without bothering to engage the full back, swung a left foot cross towards the near post. For a moment it looked as if the pass was wasted, but his club colleague Geoff Hurst knew this script off by heart: 'I was there to meet it. We had worked for hours with West Ham on timing the run, so that you hit the space at exactly the right time.' Unmarked, Hurst headed the ball across Roma into the

ABOVE | The moment when a football match became an international incident. Referee Rudolf Kreitlein finally tired of Argentina's antics and sent off their captain, Antonio Rattin. At one stage it seemed the whole team would join him on the touchline, but eventually he was persuaded to make his way to the dressing room. After the match, the Argentines attempted to storm the England dressing room; Jack Charlton was all for letting them in.

far corner for the only goal of the game.

The final whistle was the signal for more drama. Alf Ramsey was so incensed by the way Argentina had approached the match that he stepped in to prevent George Cohen swapping his England shirt. Some of the Argentines then attempted to break down the door of the England dressing room. Jack Charlton, never one to shrink from combat, was all for letting them in. Finally came the quote for which Ramsey will always be remembered: 'We have still to produce our best football. It will come against the right type of opposition, a team who come to play football and not act as animals.'

His remarks caused a storm and were heavily criticised by the FIFA disciplinary committee, which met the following day. The committee also found that the Argentine team and officials had 'brought the game into grave disrepute', but their fine of 1,000 Swiss francs – the maximum permitted – seemed a mere slap on the wrist. Suspensions for a number of matches were announced for Rattin, Ferreiro and Onega: the latter for spitting in the face of an official. Cautions were also confirmed for Artime and Solari, and – a rarity this one – for both Charlton brothers. FIFA also recommended Argentina be suspended from the next World Cup unless 'certain assurances are given as to the conduct of players and officials.' In

ABOVE RIGHT | Antonio Rattin encounters an English stiff upper lip on a sightseeing tour of London. The FIFA committee suspended a number of Argentine players following the infamous quarter-final, but also censured Alf Ramsey for his remark that England would perform better against a team which did not 'act as animals'.

RIGHT | Jimmy Greaves relaxes with a James Bond novel. A genius on the field, his mischievous character and sharp wit endeared him to all the England players.

fact they were later allowed to take part in the 1970 competition, but finished bottom of their qualifying group.

Meanwhile the other South American quarter-finalists, Uruguay, had two men sent off in their 4–0 defeat by West Germany. The Germans would now play the USSR, who had squeezed past Hungary, 2–1. In the other match at Goodison Park, the North Koreans led Portugal 3–0 at one stage, only for Eusebio to restore normal service. He scored four times, including two penalties, as his team eventually triumphed 5–3, and qualified to meet England in the semi-final.

FIFA now had another decision to make. Originally it was understood that the second semi-final would be played at Goodison Park. However, with England now in the last four, FIFA ruled that the matches should be switched, with England v Portugal moved to Wembley for its greater capacity. Though the decision made sense in financial terms, it did nothing to ease the feeling of some countries that the host nation had waived the rules.

On Monday 25 July, West Germany reached the final for the second time by beating the USSR 2–1 at Goodison. Franz Beckenbauer

LEFT | Nobby Stiles – without his customary lenses – tries his hand at bowling and batting during training at Roehampton. Behind the stumps Martin Peters, a fine schoolboy cricketer, is unimpressed.

'THERE WAS A LATE SCARE IN THE ENGLAND DRESSING ROOM WHEN GORDON BANKS FOUND THERE WAS NO CHEWING GUM'

was again the outstanding German player, and scored what turned out to be the winning goal. He was also booked for the second time in the competition, but manager Helmut Schoen believed he would still be eligible for the final. The German boss later defended his team against accusations of play acting after the Russians had Chislenko sent off – the fourth player to be dismissed against the Germans in five matches.

England's semi-final the following evening turned out to be one of the best matches of the entire tournament. For that the Portuguese deserved much credit: *The Daily Mail* reckoned they managed thirty-two attempts on goal compared with their opponents' nineteen, and earned thirteen corners to only seven by England.

Before the kick off there was a late scare in the England dressing room when Gordon Banks found there was no chewing gum. He had learned a trick from the famous German goalkeeper Bert Trautmann, who would chew a little gum and then spit on his hands to make them stickier. In his autobiography, Banks recalls the pre-match panic: 'Poor old Harold Shepherdson was despatched by Alf to a paper shop at the very end of Wembley Way. The teams were in the tunnel by the time he'd run back, exhausted, into the stadium with his arm raised high to show he'd got my gum.'

With Greaves still out, Ramsey chose the eleven which had beaten Argentina, and finally his team found the fluency that had been absent so far. Nobby Stiles was asked to shackle Eusebio, as he had done twice for Manchester United against Benfica earlier in the season. George Cohen said later that the FA should have released a film of how Stiles performed against such a lethal opponent: anticipating his movements, and shepherding him away from goal whenever possible. A delighted Ramsey singled him out for praise in the dressing room afterwards.

But the man of the match was Bobby Charlton, who, in his finest display for his country, scored both of England's goals. Roger Hunt had a big part in the first after thirty-one minutes, chasing a ball into the Portuguese penalty area and forcing goalkeeper Pereira to parry with his feet. The ball came out to Charlton on the edge of

RIGHT | In marked contrast to the quarter-final, England's semi-final with Portugal was played in a fine spirit. At the end of the match Eusebio, who was the top scorer in the 1966 finals, congratulates Bobby Charlton on the two goals which took England into the final.

OVERLEAF | The England team wait by their bus after another training session at Roehampton. Despite their protests, Alf Ramsey insisted that the players made the hour's journey each day from their hotel in north London. Already aboard is Jimmy Greaves, who – with England in the final – would now become the subject of a fierce debate about whether he should be recalled to the team.

the area and he cleverly side-footed it into the centre of the goal.

The second came ten minutes from time when the persistent Hurst held off a defender in the penalty area and laid the ball back for Charlton to thump it first time past Pereira. Such was the spirit in which this game was played that, as well as the England players, one or two of the Portuguese team also congratulated the goalscorer.

There was still time for Portugal to earn a penalty kick when Jack Charlton handled on the line to prevent a goalbound Torres header. Gordon Banks was certain Eusebio would place the ball to his right: 'But then I saw Alan Ball frantically pointing that way, and, while Eusebio was waiting to take the penalty, he spotted what was happening. So I changed my mind and dived left, as the ball went to my right. It was the first goal I'd conceded. I could have strangled Bally.'

England hung on to win 2–1, and Eusebio walked off the pitch in tears. Ramsey told the press: 'This was England's greatest victory since I became manager. We have a very good side and they have done all that was asked of them. It should be an extremely good final, but I do not think West Germany will provide a greater challenge than Portugal did tonight.'

ALAN BALL

ONE APRIL evening in 2007, Alan Ball went to check on the small fire he had started in his back garden. He suffered a heart attack, and was found dead a short time later by firemen. He was sixty-one, the youngest of the eleven players who beat West Germany in July 1966. Jack Charlton wept at his funeral, and he was not the only one. They all loved him. They loved him because he liked a laugh, and with that unmistakeable high-pitched voice was the life and soul of any party. They loved him too because he was afraid of no one, however many caps they had won. Above all they loved him for his desire to be the best, and on that sunny day at Wembley he was the best, 'running himself daft' in Kenneth Wolstenhome's phrase and, at twenty-one years old, was Man of the Match.

Ball's father, Alan Ball Senior, here with his son, had played at a lower league level but was determined that his son would achieve greater things. Every night at their home near Bolton there would be an hour's training with a football. As a schoolboy Ball lacked height and strength. The Bolton Wanderers manager Bill Ridding told him that 'The only apprenticeship you'll get is as a jockey.' But Blackpool recognised the energy within, and in August 1962 he made his first team debut at Anfield.

In goal for Blackpool that day was Tony Waiters: 'Alan was only seventeen, but fearless. He'd already told Stanley Matthews in a practice match to f…..g run for the ball instead of expecting it to his feet all the time. None of us could believe it. Stanley Matthews for God's sake! That day against Liverpool, the place was heaving because it was their first match back in the First Division. We were so nervous we actually kicked in at the Kop End by mistake. But I saved a penalty, we won 2–1 and Bally strutted round Anfield as if he owned the place.'

Ball had told his father that he would play for England before his twentieth birthday. He made it with three days to spare when Ramsey picked him against Yugoslavia in May 1965, the first of his seventy-two caps. Ball was always highly appreciative of the England manager: 'Alf was an intensely loyal man. You never took anything for granted, but if you put the effort in on the pitch, he would pick you.'

That loyalty was tested only once, when after the opening match of the 1966 finals, Ramsey left him out for the next two games. By his own admission, Ball moped like a spoilt boy, only for his spirits to recover when the manager told him before the quarter-final that 'I've a job for you tomorrow. Argentina have an attacking left back called Marzolini, and he won't be able to attack if you are there.' Ball defused his opponent, and kept his place. In the final an even better full back, Karl Heinz Schnellinger, was virtually out on his feet in extra time, tormented by Ball's constant probing.

It was inevitable that Ball would leave Blackpool that summer. His father negotiated his contract once they had chosen to turn down Don Revie at Leeds, and instead join Everton for £110,000. At Goodison, he formed a partnership with Colin Harvey and Howard Kendall that, in the eyes of Everton fans, approached sainthood. He gave further good service to both Arsenal and Southampton, but like so many of his 1966 colleagues, was unsuccessful as a manager. He could sympathise with players who lacked his talent, but not those who failed to match his desire.

His wife Lesley died in 2004 after a long battle with cancer. They had been childhood sweethearts, and in his autobiography Ball paid tribute to her bravery and sense of fairness: 'She had worked everything out, and even asked me to sell my World Cup medal so that all three of our kids could benefit. It was a terrible time in my life, but when I look back at my football career I was lucky. I played at a time when players were still close to the people. Now they drive cars with blacked out windows, and hire whole clubs for a night out. We were just ordinary, approachable people.'

THE MAN who produced the 1966 World Cup final coverage for the BBC had one regret. The match, which attracted a record TV audience of more than thirty-two million, should have been shot and transmitted in colour. Alec Weeks, who died in 2011, always believed colour sets could have been manufactured in time for the World Cup, instead of first appearing on the market the following year. Colour newsreel footage was later available, and the documentary Goal was made in colour, but the live pictures of the thirty-two matches produced by the consortium of BBC and ITV for the tournament were in black and white only.

Nevertheless TV production of the 1966 event was a huge improvement on the coverage in Chile four years earlier, which was only seen in the UK two days later once the match film had been flown back, processed and edited.

Now electronic cameras were the norm, together with videotape editing, and, for the first time in the UK, a slow-motion/stop-action machine was purchased by the BBC for £58,000 – a huge sum in those days. However, only today's goal-line technology could determine if Geoff Hurst's second goal in the final actually crossed the line. Outside broadcast cameras of the time required two men to lift them: these days a small 'effects' camera – on the side of a pole vault bar, for instance – would fit into the palm of one hand. Away from Wembley, most games were covered by four or five cameras, but for the final Weeks used ten; today's FA Cup final would probably require three times that number.

In 1966, not only were there no dedicated sports channels, but there were only three channels in total serving the British public – BBC One, ITV and the fledgling service BBC Two, the home of Match of the Day. The famous football programme, which began in August 1964, was gradually been rolled out to other parts of the country, and showed only highlights. Indeed, whereas there are now often three live matches a day on TV channels, in the early 1960s only three matches a year were normally shown live – the FA Cup Final, England v Scotland and a European club final.

TV & RADIO...

It was perhaps no surprise therefore that ITV in the main limited their live coverage of the 1966 finals to England matches only. Regular shows like Emergency Ward 10 or Coronation Street took precedence over football, and highlights of other matches were shown only after 10.30 p.m. ITV's live transmission of the England versus France match began thirty minutes into the match, but arrived just in time to see Roger Hunt's first goal.

The BBC, whose team is pictured here, embraced the tournament more fully. As well as England matches, they chose to show other games live, including the epic Brazil v Hungary match on 15 July. To be fair, the TV companies were not helped by the simultaneous start times: all four games in the quarter-finals on Saturday, 23 July 23rd, for instance, kicked off at 3 p.m.

The main BBC commentator was Kenneth Wolstenhome, while David Coleman was used as both commentator and presenter of programmes during the event. Other BBC 'voices' were Walley Barnes, Frank Bough and Alan Weeks. The Radio Times also introduced the line-up of BBC experts, which included Billy Wright, Danny Blanchflower and Tommy Docherty (who tipped West Germany to win the final). Brian Moore, later to join ITV with such distinction, Alan Clarke, Maurice Edelston and Simon Smith were the main radio commentators.

For the benefit of newer viewers, the magazine tried to explain the 4-3-3 formation: 'Just remember the shirt numbers are purely for identification.

The midfield and forward trios will keep whirling around like a spinning top, and the flank defenders will dart into the attack like old fashioned wingmen.' So that's what Ramsey intended!

The TV Times preview unashamedly put entertainment before football know-how, and published the forecasts of DJ Pete Murray, Dusty Springfield and Ken Dodd. At the time ITV only had one full-time football commentator, Gerry Loftus, and had to carry out a number of auditions. One of the triallists was Barry Davies: 'A few of us were asked to commentate, for ten minutes each, on a Youth Clubs' Cup Final at the Crystal Palace Recreation Centre. I was new to it all, but had earlier written to both clubs to provide some biographies and photos, and I think the extra homework helped convince ITV.

'Along with John Camkin and Hugh Johns, I was chosen for the World Cup. My first match – USSR versus North Korea – was only my third proper TV commentary. The North Koreans were very friendly and let us watch them train. I thought I knew all their faces well, until I realized that Yang Sung Kook, who played in the famous match against Italy, had been given a crew cut since posing for their team picture.'

Later, of course, Davies joined the BBC, and was the commentator on the 1994 World Cup Final, but in 1966 he watched the final from the back of Hugh Johns' commentary box. Johns was unfortunate in that his words at the end of the match have been overshadowed by those of the BBC's Wolstenhome. As Hurst bore down on the German goal to score his third goal, Johns said, 'Here's Hurst. He might make it three. He has. He has. So that's it. That ... is ... it.'

Wolstenhome's verdict has become part of football's folklore: 'And here's comes Hurst. He's got ... Some people are on the pitch. They think it's all over. It is now. It's four!'

GEOFF HURST

ANYONE WHO knows football can quote the BBC commentary as, with seconds left in the match, Geoff Hurst's left foot shot made him the only man so far to score a hat-trick in a World Cup final. 'They think it's all over … it is now' has been replayed a million times.

This was not the moment that Hurst realised the extent of what he'd done, however. For one thing, he was not certain the goal had counted, so while his colleagues celebrated, he stepped out of the dressing room briefly to check that the scoreboard had registered the fourth England goal. Nor was it his appearance later on the balcony of the Royal Garden Hotel, as the huge crowd chanted the names of their England heroes. 'It was actually the following day,' remembered Hurst, 'when this huge limousine came to take me to a function, and actually cast a shadow over our little house in Hornchurch.'

'But it didn't last long. I came back home and mowed the lawn. That's what you did on a Sunday. Life went on. Remember, this was the end of July, and three weeks later I was back playing for West Ham in the first match of the season against Chelsea. The only big change to my life was that, having earned about £45 a week before the World Cup, the club doubled my wages.'

At one stage, even a regular first-team spot with the Hammers seemed beyond Hurst. Born near Manchester in 1941, his family moved south when his father, Charlie, who had played for a number of league clubs, joined Chelmsford City. As a schoolboy, Hurst had a good academic record as well as a sporting one, and for a time appeared to be making more progress as a cricketer. Even after joining West Ham and making his debut as wing half in 1960, he was chosen to play for the Essex first team against Lancashire.

In September 1962 the West Ham manager Ron Greenwood, whose team had won only a single point from their first five matches, persuaded Hurst to play up front against Liverpool. The match was won, and Hurst had found his true role, forming a fruitful partnership over the next few seasons with the club's record signing, Johnny Byrne. Wembley victories in the FA Cup and European Cup Winners' Cup followed.

In December 1965 Hurst was called into the England squad for the match against Poland. In training, Alf Ramsey noticed that the new boy was holding back a little and reminded him quietly that he had been picked on merit. 'It made me realise that I had to have a good attitude on and off the pitch,' said Hurst. 'Later there were players picked for the squad, but not for an actual match, because Alf had noticed something about their attitude which didn't fit.'

Ramsey selected Hurst for his debut in February 1966 against West Germany, and in the next match against Scotland he scored his first goal for England. When the shirt numbers were announced before the summer tour, Hurst was allotted number ten, but performed poorly in the match against Denmark and was left out of the opening game of the finals: 'Quite honestly, I watched the Uruguay game sitting next to Martin Peters and felt happy just to be there. But then Jimmy Greaves got injured and I was the only other striker in the squad.'

Hurst's clever header in the quarter-final, and his all-round performance in the semi-final against Portugal meant there was no way back for Greaves. Though he knew and appreciated Jimmy Greaves' record, Hurst said

later he could not feel sympathetic: 'Jimmy is a lovely guy and was a great, great player. But in football if you're in, you're in, and the same if you're out. There's never any sympathy. That's simply part and parcel of being a professional footballer.'

If anything, Hurst became an even better player after 1966. He went on to win forty-nine caps for England, including the finals four years later in Mexico. West Ham turned down an offer of £200,000 from Manchester United for him in 1968, and it was not until 1972 that he left the club for Stoke, followed by a short spell at West Bromwich Albion.

After retiring as a player, he managed Telford, and then Chelsea for two seasons before being sacked in 1981. 'Coaching was the easy bit,' he told the BBC later, 'but behind the scenes at Stamford Bridge things were difficult. I told my wife, Judith, I'd had enough of football and pulled the curtain down hard.' Hurst then pursued a successful career in the motor-insurance business, but later came back into football, working with companies to promote better coaching for children, and acted as a bid ambassador on the FA's campaign to bring the World Cup finals to England in 2006.

Knighted for services to football and now well into his seventies, Hurst remains in demand. The world still wants to discuss his hat-trick, and whether his second goal was over the line or not. He admits to a slightly guilty feeling of relief when the Frenchman Zinedine Zidane failed to add to his two first-half goals in the 1998 World Cup final.

At the time of the 1966 event it was customary for the scorer of a hat-trick to be awarded the match ball, but play never resumed after the final goal and Hurst never recovered it. The now-famous orange ball was eventually taken home to Germany by Helmut Haller. Thirty years later he was persuaded to return it, after the *Daily Mirror* offered him £80,000 for possession of the ball and asked Hurst to be on hand to receive it. But *The Sun* also wanted the ball, and it was only after a frantic helicopter chase across the country that Hurst finally held the ball – for a few minutes – in his hands.

'Was it the real ball? I think so,' said Hurst later. 'The leather was in reasonable condition, though the bladder was deflated. If I had been given the ball in the first place it would probably have sat untouched in a dusty cupboard. This way everyone seemed happy.'

11: CORONATION
30 JULY 1966

Jimmy Greaves in action against an Arsenal eleven, in a match to decide his fitness, if selected, for the final against West Germany. With no substitutes allowed, Ramsey had to decide whether to bring back England's record goalscorer or preserve a winning team.

THE DAILY COACH JOURNEY FROM THE HENDON HALL HOTEL TO THE ENGLAND TRAINING CAMP AT ROEHAMPTON WAS LONG AND TIRESOME FOR THE PLAYERS.

Some time earlier, Bobby Charlton had been 'volunteered' to ask Ramsey to consider a more adjacent venue. But, as with the players' request about the suits, the manager promised to think about it, told them he had done and then announced that they would still travel to Roehampton.

With the final four days away, however, there was a change of sorts. Ramsey spared the eleven who had beaten Portugal, allowing them to watch the rest of the squad tackle a tough practice match against Arsenal at London Colney. All were all aware of the real reason for the game: to examine the mind and body of Jimmy Greaves. He had missed the last two games with an ugly gash to his shin from the French match. Jack Charlton recalls seeing him on the treatment table: 'His leg was all blue and yellow. I pretended I was going to touch it and Jim nearly jumped off the table. At that time there were no substitutes in the World Cup, remember, so you had to be absolutely certain that you would last the ninety minutes. Otherwise, Alf wouldn't pick you.'

Against Arsenal, Greaves looked sharp as the England 'second eleven' won 3–1, and then chaired captain Jimmy Armfield off the field. The question was should the Spurs striker now be recalled for the final? And, if so, whom should Ramsey leave out? The argument for the return of Greaves was easily made. Before the finals he had scored forty-three goals for England in fifty-four matches. Those who faced him on a regular basis in the First Division were aware of the damage he could inflict, and had inflicted, ever since his debut

as a seventeen-year-old for Chelsea in 1957. Armfield had no doubt Greaves was the best finisher he'd ever seen. Norman Hunter said if you left him even for a second, he'd hurt you. Nobby Stiles called him the quickest and most natural striker in the English game.

However, even the members of this judiciary believe Ramsey would have been wrong to change course for the final. It was clear that Greaves had not been at his best in the group games and his injury had proved a blessing. Hunt had scored three goals so far, but more importantly his combination with Hurst had been a feature of England's best performance in the semi-final. Hurst's power in the air had decided the match against Argentina; his selfless lay-off had led to Charlton's second goal against Portugal. On the other hand, Hurst had played only seven times for England, and the final would be by far the biggest test of his career.

George Cohen later summed up Ramsey's dilemma: 'Jimmy was a fantastic player. No defender wanted to play against him. But he

RIGHT | Some of the wives of the England players who travelled to London for the final. L to R: Lesley Newton (Alan Ball's girlfriend), Judith Hurst, Kay Stiles, Norma Charlton, Pat Wilson, Carol Paine and Ursula Banks.

had been ill with hepatitis and lost a yard, maybe two. When Alf saw the combination of Hunt and Hurst working so well there was no going back. At the time there was really nothing you could say to Jimmy. If you caught his eye in a hotel corridor it was difficult. He knew that, by a piece of sheer bad luck, the greatest opportunity of his career had been taken away.'

Cohen, like the rest of the defence, was certain to play. But, unknown to the rest of the squad, Bobby Moore had contracted tonsillitis. Cohen recalls overhearing Ramsey sounding out his assistants on the readiness of Norman Hunter, but the team doctor, Alan Bass, had by then ensured the captain would be fit. Four years earlier, England had travelled to Chile without a doctor, which could have had serious consequences when centre half Peter Swan became ill.

On the eve of the final, Ramsey took the squad to the cinema to see *Those Magnificent Men in their Flying Machines*, and used

the occasion to put a few minds at rest. Roger Hunt recalls that, 'We'd just got off the coach and Alf sidled up to me and said, "You are playing tomorrow. Good luck." And that was it. I didn't know who else was playing.' Ramsey had also told Hurst, but reminded him to keep silent about being selected. That was too much to ask. When he returned to the room he was sharing with his pal Peters, he could hardly contain himself, and was overjoyed to learn that Peters, too, was in the team.

A few doors along, in the room he shared with Nobby Stiles, a fretful Alan Ball had heard nothing. He believed the England manager was still pondering a role for Greaves. Early the next morning Stiles, taking care not to disturb his roommate, tiptoed out to take Mass, as he had done on every match day so far. He was not the first to rise: George Cohen was in the lobby having slept poorly, but was sufficiently awake to wish Stiles luck in finding a Catholic church in nearby Golders Green.

He needn't have worried. Stiles had wrestled with the problem already. He told James Lawton: 'Wembley was a particularly draining pitch to play on. So part of me wanted to be as well rested as possible for each match. But there was the fear that, if I changed anything, if I went missing from the back pew of the church I'd always used, I might break the spell of England winning and bring all kinds of disaster on my head.'

Stiles returned to find Ball not only awake but remonstrating with him for actually having woken him every match day by clattering about on his way to church. Soon, however, all Ball's anxieties were removed: after breakfast Ramsey told him he would play in the final, and the young man sprinted off to tell his father to fill up the Morris Minor and get himself down to Wembley.

Many journalists that morning were still acting as cheerleaders for the game-changing skills of Greaves. Every prediction underlined the enormous pressure on the manager: if England were to lose having picked Greaves, Ramsey would be chastised for changing a winning team; lose without him and he would be torn apart for ignoring such obvious talent. In the *Daily Mail* Brian James wrote: 'For three years he has held the loneliest job in sport by steering a ridiculed team and a misunderstood method this far. No one should envy him his decision.'

The player himself, though, did not need telling. Harold Sheperson had prepared the way before the England manager took him aside later that morning. There were no scenes or asides to the press. Indeed, to his great credit, Greaves refused to allow his disappointment to affect the mood of the squad. However, to his roommate Bobby Moore's surprise, he was already – both figuratively and physically – packing his bags and would depart on holiday the next evening.

Ramsey then briefed the team. Though most knew their roles already, given that the German team had been announced the

RIGHT | Martin Peters heads for the bus taking the England squad to Wembley. Having won his first cap only two months earlier, he was now about to play in the World Cup final.

previous day, there was a bombshell for Bobby Charlton: 'Alf said I want you to stay with Franz Beckenbauer the whole game. He's young and he can run, but so can you. If you prevent him doing any damage, we will win the World Cup.' Charlton's first reaction was disbelief, given that he had never man-marked anyone before,

let alone assumed a role more suited to his club colleague Stiles. Nevertheless, if Ramsey needed this job doing – and he'd been right about so much so far – Charlton would do it.

One can only imagine the intense fervour to which the nation would abandon itself if England were to reach the World Cup final in the twenty-first century. Players would be mobbed, with cameras and microphones everywhere. On the morning of the 1966 final, by contrast, Bobby Charlton and Ray Wilson were able to walk without much hindrance to the shops in Golders Green: Charlton changed a shirt he had bought earlier; Wilson purchased some shoes for the banquet after the match. A few autographs were signed for the more persistent boys, and then they strolled back.

On the journey to Wembley, however, the players felt the mood changing. The nearer they got to the stadium the more people lined the streets, their union flags waving endlessly. Someone had produced a placard nominating Nobby Stiles for prime minister. (The real one was flying back from a dinner in Washington to attend the match.)

It would be naïve to assume that some part of this emotion was not linked to memories of the Second World War, which had ended twenty-one years earlier. The players, though, understood clearly the danger of being distracted by demands that beating Germany should deliver more than a sporting victory. Let us win the World Cup – for ourselves, for our families and for England – their stance proclaimed. Let others find further significance.

Some, like Martin Peters, could have had cause to think differently. His wife Kathy's family had suffered terribly in the Blitz, when a bomb fell on a packed family house in East Ham. Her father was the sole survivor. Others, too, had relations who had fought in the war: Geoff Hurst's father-in-law had been a paratrooper in Germany. He didn't really follow football but, patriotic to the last, told his daughter, Hurst's wife, Judith, that not only would England win but that Geoff would score a hat-trick.

First Hurst and the others had to clear the England dressing room. With barely three-quarters of an hour to kick off, the place was full of squad members, FA officials and other well-wishers. The situation was most unlike Alf Ramsey. Eventually there was room to get changed, and for little superstitions to creep in. Moore liked to be the last to put his shorts on. Peters watched until he'd slid them on, and then put his own shorts on. Moore then took his off, and waited until it was time to leave for the tunnel before replacing them! Banks tied and retied his laces until the knots were precisely on the side of each boot, not at the front where he might spot them when kicking. Before the first game against Uruguay, Les Cocker had left two balls in the dressing room by mistake and had to run back to retrieve them for the warm up. The players had insisted that he repeat the error before every match.

The noise which greeted the two teams was deafening. Seeler led out West Germany, who, judging by the flurry of flags, seemed to have plenty of support. There was no formal segregation of fans. Moore was first out for England, in his seventy-third match of the season, followed by Cohen, Ball and Banks – the goalkeeper chewing gum even though, with rain around, he planned to wear

RIGHT | World heavyweight champion Muhammad Ali at Wembley before the final. He was in England preparing for his fight against Brian London, and it is unclear whether he stayed for the match itself.

OVERLEAF | 30 July. The scene outside Wembley as the coach carrying the West Germany team arrives. There was no segregation of supporters at the final, and the majority of England fans waved the Union Flag rather than the flag of St George.

I The equalizer for England. (Left) From Moore's free kick, once again Hurst has anticipated the flight of the ball and is unmarked. (Centre) His header is so firm and direct that Tilkowski has barely moved. (Right) Hurst celebrates his first goal of a perfect hat-trick – a header, a right-foot and finally a left-foot shot .

gloves. Then came Hunt, Wilson, Hurst and Bobby Charlton. Peters was next, having made the sensible decision earlier to give way to Jack Charlton, who also preferred to be last out of the tunnel. Stiles, who had removed his front teeth and asked Ian Callaghan to look after them, separated the two of them.

The two managers, Schoen and Ramsey, had both done their homework on the opposition. The Germans would play with a sweeper, Schulz, leaving Hottges and Weber to look after Hurst and Hunt respectively. The highly rated left back Schnellinger would have Ball, the youngest player on the field, for company. Late in the game, when the England number seven had again left his German marker gasping for breath, it seemed a dubious pleasure. Finally, and perhaps not surprisingly, Schoen had instructed his most gifted player, Franz Beckenbauer, to stay close to Bobby Charlton throughout. The two most creative players therefore cancelled each other out. It meant the match was tense and always interesting, but in truth lacked the quality of England's semi-final.

West Germany scored first when, in the thirteenth minute, Ray Wilson mistimed a clearing header, which dropped to Haller. Even then his shot was not well struck but still somehow found its way past both Jack Charlton and Banks and into the corner. The England players sat in the stands struggled to remember the last time

OVERLEAF | England's second goal. The ball
has spun off Hottges (far left) and Peters
volleys the ball between Tilkowski and
Schnellinger on the line. The other players are
Hunt, Weber, Jack Charlton – delighted the ball
had not fallen to him – and Overath.

Wilson had made a mistake. Above them on the TV gantry, BBC
commentator Kenneth Wolstenholme was reminding his audience
that in the previous four finals the team who scored first had
always lost.

Within minutes it was 1–1. The goal was another product of
the West Ham training ground. Moore, moving out from defence,
was fouled by Overath about forty yards from goal, but put the
ball down, looked up once and struck the free kick quickly. Hurst
had again moved early, leaving Hottges five yards adrift, and the
England striker headed easily past a static Tilkowski. That was the
way the score stayed until the interval. Overall, England probably
had the better of a jittery first half. There had been too many
stoppages and free kicks, though few for the kind of graceless fouls
practised by Argentina. The only name taken by referee Gottfried
Dienst was Martin Peters, for shirt pulling.

The start of the second period was marked with rain. England
continued to have more of the game but the shadow of Beckenbauer
was preventing Bobby Charlton repeating the contribution he had
made in the semi-final. As for West Germany, left winger Emmerich
was making little progress against Cohen; Stiles, meanwhile, was
frustrating Overath, West Germany's best player on the day, by
cutting out his service to Held and Seeler.

RIGHT | With seconds left of normal time, West Germany make the score 2–2. (Left) For Emmerich's free kick the England wall assembles but there are too many players behind it. (Centre) After the ball hits the arm of Schnellinger, it is bundled in by Weber at the far post. (Right) In vain Moore continues to claim handball to the referee, but the goal stands.

With thirteen minutes left, Ball took a corner on the right. The ball came out to Hurst on the edge of the area; his slightly scuffed shot was deflected into the air by Hottges. For a moment it seemed Jack Charlton might reach the ball first. Mercifully for England, it was Peters who arrived to volley the ball between Tilkowski and Schnellinger on the line. England now led 2–1, and should have finished the match four minutes before the end. Ball found Hunt, and, with Bobby Charlton in attendance, England suddenly had three attackers against one German. But Hunt's pass was too deliberate and too square, forcing Charlton into a snatched, inconclusive effort.

It was to prove an expensive mistake. With seconds left, and with English supporters beseeching Dienst to blow the whistle, he finally did so, but only to award Germany a free kick for a foul by Jack Charlton. The England wall was hastily assembled, with Cohen worrying there were too many bodies behind it, obstructing Banks' view. Following the free kick, Held's effort was deflected off Cohen's knee. Banks believed the ball would have run wide had it not hit the underside of Schnellinger's arm, taking the pace off it. Now it was a race to the far post. Ray Wilson stretched a leg, Banks

dived across just above him, but Weber was intelligent enough to lift the ball over them both and make the score 2–2.

With victory wrenched away, and facing a further thirty minutes of extra time, the England players now huddled together to listen to Ramsey. It was the England manager's finest hour. 'We were in turmoil after they scored, but the first thing he did was to calm us all down,' said George Cohen. 'Then he told us to look at the Germans. They are on their knees, he said. They are finished. You've won the game once, now go and win it again.'

Many of the England squad players had missed the German equaliser. They had watched from the stands, rather than the bench, knowing that Ramsey had asked them to come pitch-side, win or lose, at the end of the match.

Jimmy Armfield recalled: 'I was in the stand with the other lads. Sitting near us was Jack and Bobby's dad, who was more into pigeons than football. Anyway, with England leading 2–1 we headed for the lift down to the players' tunnel. The lift was struggling and it took us the best part of five minutes to get down. I got out just as Weber scored. Those behind me never saw the goal.'

Alf Ramsey's finest hour. With his players distraught and facing thirty minutes of extra time, the England manager told them to stand up, and then look at the Germans. 'They are finished,' he said. 'You've won it once. Go out and win the match again.'

Once extra time started, the squad squeezed in behind Ramsey and were treated to a display by Alan Ball that he may never have bettered. Nobby Stiles said later: 'Bally was absolutely brilliant. When the Germans equalised, and we were all gutted, he grabbed the ball and ran to put it on the centre spot and show them he was ready to go again. Then in extra time I went to cross the ball and nothing happened. I just couldn't run another step. But little Bally came past me and said, "Move, you little bastard," and somehow I got going again.'

No one offered such comfort to Schnellinger, who now appeared to require roller skates to deal with the threat of Ball. It was his near-post cross which reached Hurst in the tenth minute of extra time, and led to an eternal debate about whether the ball had crossed the line or not. 'The ball came slightly behind me,' Hurst said later, 'but I turned and hit it with my right foot. It hit the underside of the bar and came down, but in that split second I was falling too and probably had the worst view of anyone in the stadium.'

Many believe that the reaction of the nearest England player, Roger Hunt, remains the answer. He turned away, arm raised to claim the goal, and did not attempt to reach the rebound as any

ABOVE LEFT | Fifty years on, the legitimacy of England's third goal is still debated. The nearest England player to the goal, Roger Hunt, was certain the ball was over the line, but could not have reached the rebound in any case.

player, with doubt in his mind, would have done. Hunt himself says, 'I am still convinced it was over the line. But in fact I couldn't have reached it anyway. The ball bounced down from the bar and then went off at an angle towards the far post. Then Weber headed it away for a corner. I was on holiday once with Denis Law and even he agreed that I couldn't have reached the rebound.'

Referee Dienst wasn't certain either and decided to consult Tofik Bakhramov, the linesman from Azerbaijan. His viewpoint was thirty yards away and level with the six-yard box; his verdict was that the goal should stand. Fifty years on the decision is still debated. There was no goal-line technology, of course, and the film evidence is far from conclusive, though a recent Sky Sports initiative showed that the goal was legitimate. Ten years ago, though, a study by the department of engineering science at Oxford University found that, in their view, the ball was probably six centimetres from being wholly across the line.

Even with the goal given, those on the pitch were taking nothing for granted. There were still twenty minutes of extra time to go, and the Germans refused to lie down. When have they ever? Minutes passed, with the crowd again screaming their frustration that the

ABOVE | (Centre) With Overath in chase, Hurst puts every ounce of strength into his shot which (right) flies past Tilkowski for England's fourth goal.

RIGHT | The England coach edged its way through massed crowds in Kensington High Street on its way to the official reception and banquet.

referee's watch seemed to have selected slow motion. Then, in one of those moments in keeping with the career of Bobby Moore, the England captain nursed the ball out of defence on the left of his own penalty area. There were seconds left, and the demand from his colleague Jack Charlton, echoed by every England supporter in the stadium, was to despatch the ball into the nearest stand, and over it if possible. Instead Moore looked up and hit a perfect pass to Hurst in the inside left position. Setting off for goal, and chased by Overath, Hurst's mind was made up: 'Bally was to my right, but all I wanted to do was shoot with every ounce of my strength. I thought, even I hit it into the car park, it'll take a while to fetch it and the game will be over.'

As every English football fan knows, the ball flew past Tilkowski into the top corner. Hurst had his hat-trick, Wolstenholme had found the words to match and Dienst finally blew for time. On the bench they were already celebrating; everyone, that is, except Ramsey, who told Harold Shepherdson to sit down. On the field Ball turned cartwheels, and Stiles fell on top of Cohen like a lover possessed. Bobby Charlton, tears welling up, told his brother Jack

242 | CORONATION

ABOVE | Huge crowds gather outside the Royal Garden Hotel waiting for the England squad to appear with the Jules Rimet trophy.

that life would never be the same again. As the team climbed the steps to collect the Jules Rimet trophy, Moore remembered to wipe the sweat from his palms on the velvet counter of the Royal Box before shaking hands with the Queen.

Nobby Stiles never bothered to put his teeth back in. During the team's lap of honour he danced a little jig of delight, his grin as wide as Wembley. Moore and the others tried to persuade Ramsey to join their parade, but he refused. He was already looking ahead: 'Everyone seems to be asking me what I'm going to do,' said Ramsey afterwards. 'But there is another World Cup in four years' time in Mexico, and it would be nice to win there also.'

For the Germans, Helmut Schoen was gracious in defeat.

'England won well and we are not annoyed. The two teams fought the match in a fair way.' The Minister of Sport Denis Howell said simply, 'This has been the best half million pounds the government has ever spent.'

After leaving Wembley the whole squad returned to Hendon Hall to change, and then travelled by coach to the official banquet at the Royal Garden Hotel in Kensington, outside which enormous crowds had gathered. On the hotel balcony each player was cheered as they held up the trophy in turn. Prime Minister Harold Wilson's appearance, by contrast, received a mixture of cheers and boos.

The England players' wives and girlfriends had also been invited to the evening, but, astonishingly, were asked to dine in a separate room. Not all could make it anyway. Norman Hunter's fiancée, Susanne Harper, managed a hairdressing salon in Leeds. 'I rang her once we reached the final, and said, "Are you coming down? There's a big do after the match." She said, "No, I've got hair to cut." Some people would have killed to be there, but she felt she couldn't let her customers down.'

Another absentee was Jimmy Greaves, who slipped away before dinner was served. 'My overwhelming feeling that day was being

ABOVE | (Left) Tina Moore models the dress she wore for the evening's celebrations. (Right) The players' wives, however, were asked to dine in a separate room from their husbands.

ABOVE | Bobby Charlton at the post-match banquet. His role in the final typified Ramsey's winning formula, sacrificing individual performance for the sake of the team.

the loneliest man at Wembley. All I wanted to do was go away and be alone. I couldn't force myself to join the festivities. I always thought we would win the World Cup. I just never thought we'd win it without me.'

After the formal part of the evening, the players were finally released to join their wives and venture out into the West End. The various couples found they were welcomed at the Playboy or Danny La Rue's Club. Jack Charlton's wife, Pat, was at home expecting the birth of their second son, so he was alone. He had, however, acquired another trophy earlier to go with his winner's medal: 'As we came off the pitch at Wembley, I was asked to give a urine sample. I said "not again" because I'd been picked after four of the six games. I was there for ages and they had to ply me with drinks before anything happened. At the end the doctors presented me with this plastic potty, shaped like a bowler hat, and in big letters they'd written "For one who gave his best for England – the Jimmy Riddle Trophy!"'

RG

THE FOOTBALL ASSOCIATION

World Championship Jules Rimet Cup

BANQUET

in honour of
F. I. F. A.
and
The Teams Competing in
The Finals

———

ROYAL GARDEN HOTEL
LONDON

———

Saturday, 30th July, 1966

TOAST LIST

HER MAJESTY THE QUEEN

———

PRESIDENTS & HEADS OF STATES HERE REPRESENTED

THE FOOTBALL ASSOCIATION

Proposed by
SIR STANLEY ROUS, C.B.E.

Response by
The Rt. Hon. THE EARL OF HAREWOOD, LL.D.

———

PRESENTATION OF MEDALS AND GIFTS

MENU

Melon Frappé

———

Filets de Sole Veronique

———

Entrecôte Sauté Marchand de Vins
Haricots Verts au Beurre
Pommes Croquettes

———

Soufflé en Surprise Milady
Bombe Glacée World Cup
Mignardises

———

Café

———

WINES

Chablis Châtain, 1 er Cru, 1963

Gevrey Chambertin, 1961

Champagne Henkel Tröcken
(by courtesy of Henkel (London) Limited)

Cognac - Liqueurs

AUTOGRAPHS

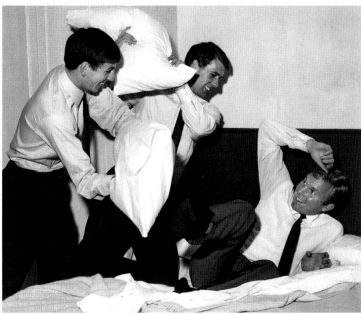

ABOVE | The West Ham trio in playful mood on and off the pitch. West Ham fans delight in recalling that in Hurst and Peters they provided the England goalscorers in the final and that Bobby Moore was named player of the tournament.

LEFT | The menu for the official banquet. It has been signed by twenty-one of Ramsey's squad, the exception being Jimmy Greaves, who went home earlier. 'I always thought we would win the World Cup,' he said later.' I just never thought they would win it without me.'

The *Sunday Express* journalist James Mossop was a good friend of Charlton's, and they met by chance outside the hotel. 'I was about to go back to Manchester,' said Mossop, 'but Jack said, "No, you are coming out with me."' The two men went to the Astor Club, known to a few of the England players. After more drinks, a complete stranger called Lenny asked them to join him. 'Eventually Jack and I agreed to go back to his place in Walthamstow and carry on. We slept on his sofa, and when we woke up the next day a lady shouts to Jack over the garden wall. It turns out she's a neighbour of his from Ashington!'

Charlton had taken the precaution of carrying a note saying 'Please return this body' and the name and room number of his hotel. But when he found his way back, he discovered that his mother had been worried because his bed had not been slept in. 'She was not at all happy I'd gone missing,' said Jack, 'but I had to laugh. I was thirty-one years of age, I'd just won the World Cup, and my mother's yelling at me for staying out late!'

CONCLUSION

The 1966 World Cup finals in England were undoubtedly a commercial success. The receipts for the final were a world record £204,805, and total tickets sales for the tournament were more than £1.5 million. Some estimates put the FA's profit at around £3 million – an enormous sum in those days. However, due to some poor financial planning, the organisation was forced to pay tax of almost £250,000. The players were asked to share a bonus of less than a tenth of that sum, £22,000, for winning the trophy, and agreed it should be evenly divided among the whole squad.

One can only guess at the abundance on offer should England's World Cup victory be repeated in the 21st century. The division of spoils in 1966 was entirely in keeping with the spirit instilled by Ramsey, that the team was greater than any individual, however talented. As the nation rejoiced, some moaned that Ramsey had stifled flair, and encouraged industry above elegance. The truth was that he demanded both; in Bobby Charlton he had a player who could change the course of a match in an instant, but one whose shirt at the end of each match would be damp with sweat.

Ramsey himself, whose FA contract of £4,500 a year was up for renewal the following May, was already looking ahead. He told the *Daily Mail*: 'I think we have got all we could get from this present team. My one fear for this World Cup was that we had not caught up the rest of the world enough. This victory seems to prove we have caught up, but we have to stay in front. We have got to experiment now that we have got rid of the set ideas that have ruled our game for a hundred years.'

However, in the same article, the newly appointed Football League chairman, Len Shipman, warned: 'We cannot let England have our players more freely. We share their success but the players are the club's assets, and they will now want first call on their services for club games and summer tours. It has simply got to be that way.'

England's win, for a time, made football fashionable. Politicians, newspaper editors and advertisers all fought to associate themselves with the game and its players. In the 1967 New Year's Honours List, Alf Ramsey was knighted and Bobby Moore given an OBE. There were honours, too, for the FA secretary Denis Follows and for 'World Cup Willie', the organising committee's Ken Willson. Over the years, other members of the eleven also received honours, including a knighthood for Bobby Charlton, and later Geoff Hurst. But it was not until 2000 that the 'forgotten five' – Alan Ball, George Cohen, Roger Hunt, Nobby Stiles and Ray Wilson – received the MBE from the Queen, thirty-four years after she had last shaken hands with them all.

The 1966 finals had finished later than usual, and the players were back in league action just three weeks later. Cohen's first match was against Everton, who fielded not only Wilson but also Ball, recently signed from Blackpool. By the end of the season, Stiles and Bobby Charlton had won another championship with Manchester United and Jack Charlton had been named Footballer of the Year. Gordon Banks had left for Stoke City because Leicester preferred a younger goalkeeper called Peter Shilton. At one stage Banks seemed certain to join Moore, Hurst and Peters at West Ham, but the move fell through.

For many of the squad, 1966 marked the end of their international careers. George Eastham joined Stoke even before Banks, in August 1966, and six years later – aged 35 – scored the winning goal in the League Cup Final. John Connelly, who died in 2012, left Manchester United for second division Blackburn Rovers early in the new season, and would later run a successful fish and chip shop, Connelly's Plaice.

At the end of the 1966/7 season, Ron Flowers had won promotion with Wolves while Jimmy

Armfield suffered relegation with Blackpool. Terry Paine was ever present for Southampton, and would eventually amass a record 808 appearances for the club. Ron Springett, who died in 2015, left Sheffield Wednesday for QPR in May 1967, in a swap deal involving his younger brother Peter. Gerry Byrne, who also died in 2015, missed most of the 66/7 season with injury, and never added to his two England caps.

As for Jimmy Greaves, contrary to myth, he did not descend into alcoholism as a result of his disappointment. In fact his form for Spurs was good: he scored thirty-one cup and league goals, and won an FA Cup winner's medal. He was also recalled to the England side, playing in the defeat by Scotland in April 1967, but made his final international appearance the following month against Austria. His final tally was forty-four goals in fifty-seven England matches.

In March 1970, Greaves was transferred to West Ham as part of the deal in which Peters joined Spurs, and as usual scored on his debut. But by then the drinking was becoming serious, and he retired from football at the end of the following season. To his everlasting credit, Greaves 'finally came out of my alcoholic haze' and began a new and successful career with ITV, including the Saturday lunchtime show *Saint and Greavsie* with Ian St John. He remains philosophical about missing the final – 'my greatest disappointment as a player obviously, but not the hardest thing I've had to bear in life, not by a long way.'

Of those who did play in the final, eight were in Alf Ramsey's squad in Mexico in 1970, though Stiles and Jack Charlton were no longer first choice. By then Hunt had told Ramsey he no longer wished to be considered for England, and Cohen and Wilson had retired from the game altogether. Two other squad members – Peter Bonetti and Norman Hunter – also played in Mexico four years later. But Ron Springett, Jimmy Armfield, Gerry Byrne, Ron Flowers, Terry Paine, John Connelly and George Eastham never played for England again after 1966. Ian Callaghan, by contrast, was given his third international cap by manager Ron Greenwood – eleven years later!

The players still see each other from time to time. Sadly some of those occasions have been funerals, including those for Bobby Moore and Alan Ball. Sir Alf Ramsey died in 1999, his later years frustrated by the onset of Alzheimer's and bitterness about his dismissal by the Football Association in 1974. It is not the purpose of this book to examine in detail what happened to English football after 1966, but certainly those who won the World Cup feel he was poorly treated. At the funeral in Ipswich, George Cohen said, 'His strength and purpose made it so easy to believe in him … we are here to celebrate a great manager, but also a great Englishman.'

Since England's triumph on that July afternoon in 1966, there have been twelve World Cup tournaments. In that time England have reached just one semi-final; West Germany, now Germany, have played nine, reached six finals, and won the World Cup three times. So when the players do gather for their annual reunion, as well as the laughter and the latest news of knees and hips, the talk is of the present set-up and why, for all the fortunes paid to today's England stars, they have so far failed to match the 'Boys of '66'. After fifty years, it remains a pretty exclusive club.

THE ENGLAND '40'

GOALKEEPERS

Gordon Banks	*Leicester City*
Tony Waiters	*Blackpool*
Gordon West	*Everton*
Ron Springett	*Sheffield Wednesday*
Peter Bonetti	*Chelsea*

FULL BACKS

Jimmy Armfield	*Blackpool*
Chris Lawler	*Liverpool*
Gerry Byrne	*Liverpool*
Ray Wilson	*Everton*
Paul Reaney	*Leeds United*
Keith Newton	*Blackburn Rovers*
George Cohen	*Fulham*

HALF BACKS

Norman Hunter	*Leeds United*
Gordon Milne	*Liverpool*
Ron Flowers	*Wolverhampton Wanderers*
Bobby Moore	*West Ham United*
Jack Charlton	*Leeds United*
Martin Peters	*West Ham United*
Tommy Smith	*Liverpool*
John Hollins	*Chelsea*
Marvin Hinton	*Chelsea*
Nobby Stiles	*Manchester United*

FORWARDS

John Connelly	*Manchester United*
Joe Baker	*Nottingham Forest* *
Alan Ball	*Blackpool*
Ian Callaghan	*Liverpool*
Jimmy Greaves	*Tottenham Hotspur*
Gordon Harris	*Burnley*
John Kaye	*West Bromwich Albion*
Geoff Hurst	*West Ham United*
Bobby Charlton	*Manchester United*
Terry Paine	*Southampton*
Derek Temple	*Everton*
Peter Osgood	*Chelsea*
George Eastham	*Arsenal*
Peter Thompson	*Liverpool*
Roger Hunt	*Liverpool*
Terry Venables	*Chelsea*
Barry Bridges	*Chelsea*
Fred Pickering	*Everton*

* previously with *Arsenal*

There were three new players named in the squad to train at Lilleshall: Labone (*Everton*) for Hinton, Tambling (*Chelsea*) for Bridges and Byrne (*West Ham*) for Pickering. Labone later withdrew, and so the twenty-seven were made up of the final twenty-two plus Newton, Milne, Byrne, Tambling and Thompson.

ENGLAND'S FULL INTERNATIONAL TEAMS 1963–66

+ Denotes captain • Numbers after player denote goals scored • Number after substitute denotes the player replaced

SEASON 1962-3	Result	1	2	3	4	5	6	7	8	9	10	11	Substitutes
France	2 - 5	Springett R.	Armefield +	Henry	Moore	Labone	Flowers	Connelly	Tambling1	Smith R.1	Greaves	Charlton R.	
Scotland	1 - 2	Banks G.	Armefield +	Byrne G.	Moore	Norman	Flowers	Douglas1	Greaves	Smith R.	Melia	Charlton R.	
Brazil	1 - 1	Banks G.	Armefield +	Wilson	Milne	Norman	Moore	Douglas1	Greaves	Smith R.	Eastham	Charlton R.	
Czechoslovakia	4 - 2	Banks G.	Shellito	Wilson	Milne	Norman	Moore +	Paine	Greaves2	Smith R.1	Eastham	Charlton R.1	
German D. R.	2 - 1	Banks G.	Armefield +	Wilson	Milne	Norman	Moore	Paine	Hunt1	Smith R.	Eastham	Charlton R.1	
Switzerland	8 - 1	Springett R.	Armefield +	Wilson	Kay1	Moore	Flowers	Douglas1	Greaves	Byrne J.2	Melia1	Charlton R.3	
1963-64													
Wales	4 - 0	Banks G.	Armefield +	Wilson	Milne	Norman	Moore	Paine	Greaves1	Smith R.2	Eastham	Charlton R.1	
Rest of the World	2 - 1	Banks G.	Armefield +	Wilson	Milne	Norman	Moore	Paine1	Greaves1	Smith R.	Eastham	Charlton R.	
Ireland	8 - 3	Banks G.	Armefield +	Thomson R.	Milne	Norman	Moore	Paine3	Greaves4	Smith R.1	Eastham	Charlton R.	
Scoltand	0 - 1	Banks G.	Armefield +	Wilson	Milne	Norman	Moore	Paine	Hunt	Byrne J.	Eastham	Charlton R.	
Uruguay	2 - 1	Banks G.	Cohen	Wilson	Milne	Norman	Moore +	Paine	Greaves	Byrne J. 2	Eastham	Charlton R.	
Portugal	4 - 3	Banks G.	Cohen	Wilson	Milne	Norman	Moore +	Thompson P.	Greaves	Byrne J. 3	Eastham	Charlton R.1	
Republic of Ireland	3 - 1	Waiters	Cohen	Wilson	Milne	Flowers	Moore +	Thompson P.	Greaves1	Byrne J. 1	Eastham1	Charlton R.	
U.S.A	10 - 0	Banks G.	Cohen	Thomson R.	Bailey M.	Norman	Flowers +	Paine2	Hunt4	Pickering3	Eastham	Thompson P.	Charlton R. (10)1
Brazil	1 - 5	Waiters	Cohen	Wilson	Milne	Norman	Moore +	Thompson P.	Greaves1	Byrne J.	Eastham	Charlton R.	
Portugal	1 - 1	Banks G.	Thomson R.	Wilson	Flowers	Norman	Moore +	Paine	Greaves	Byrne J.	Hunt^1	Thompson P.	
Argentina	0 - 1	Banks G.	Thomson R.	Wilson	Milne	Norman	Moore +	Thompson P.	Greaves	Byrne J.	Eastham	Charlton R.	
1964-65													
Ireland	4 - 3	Banks G.	Cohen	Thomson R.	Milne	Norman	Moore +	Paine	Greaves3	Pickering1	Charlton R.	Thompson P.	
Belgium	2 - 2	Waiters	Cohen	Thomson R.	Milne	Norman	Moore +	Thompson P.	Greaves	Pickering1	Venables	Hinton A.	
Wales	2 - 1	Waiters	Cohen	Thomson R.	Bailey M.	Flowers +	Young	Thompson P.	Hunt	Wignall2	Byrne J.	Hinton A.	
Netherlands	1 - 1	Waiters	Cohen	Thomson R.	Mullery	Norman	Flowers +	Thompson P.	Greaves1	Wignall	Venables	Charlton R.	
Scotland	2 - 2	Banks G.	Cohen	Wilson	Stiles	Charlton J.	Moore +	Thompson P.	Greaves1	Bridges	Byrne J.	Charlton R.1	
Hungary	1 - 0	Banks G.	Cohen	Wilson	Stiles	Charlton J.	Moore +	Paine	Greaves1	Bridges	Eastham	Connelly	
Yugoslavia	1 - 1	Banks G.	Cohen	Wilson	Stiles	Charlton J.	Moore +	Paine	Greaves	Bridges1	Ball	Connelly	
West Germany	1 - 0	Banks G.	Cohen	Wilson	Flowers	Charlton J.	Moore +	Paine1	Ball	Jones M.	Eastham	Temple	
Sweden	2 - 1	Banks G.	Cohen	Wilson	Stiles	Charlton J.	Moore +	Paine	Ball1	Jones M.	Eastham	Connelly^1	
1965-66													
Wales	0 - 0	Springett R.	Cohen	Wilson	Stiles	Charlton J.	Moore +	Paine	Greaves	Peacock	Charlton R.	Connelly	
Austria	2 - 3	Springett R.	Cohen	Wilson	Stiles	Charlton J.	Moore +	Paine	Greaves	Bridges	Charlton R.1	Connelly1	
Ireland	2 - 1	Banks G.	Cohen	Wilson	Stiles	Charlton J.	Moore +	Thompson P.	Baker1	Peacock1	Charlton R.	Connely	
Spain	2 - 0	Banks G.	Cohen	Wilson	Stiles	Charlton J.	Moore +	Ball	Hunt1	Baker1	Eastham	Charlton R.	Hunter (9)
Poland	1 - 1	Banks G.	Cohen	Wilson	Stiles	Charlton J.	Moore +1	Ball	Hunt	Baker	Eastham	Harris G.	
West Germany	1 - 0	Banks G.	Cohen	Newton K.	Moore +	Charlton J.	Hunter	Ball	Hunt	Stiles1	Hurst G.	Charlton R.	Wilson (3)
Scotland	4 - 3	Banks G.	Cohen	Newton K.	Stiles	Charlton J.	Moore +	Ball	Hunt2	Charlton R.1	Hurst G.1	Connelly	
Yugoslavia	2 - 0	Banks G.	Armefield +	Wilson	Peters	Charlton J.	Hunter	Paine	Greaves1	Charlton R.1	Hurst G.	Tambling	
Finland	3 - 0	Banks G.	Armefield +	Wilson	Peters1	Charlton J.	Hunter	Callaghan	Hunt1	Charlton R.	Hurst G.	Ball	
Norway	6 - 1	Springett R.	Cohen	Byrne G.	Stiles	Flowers	Moore +1	Paine	Greaves4	Charlton R.	Hunt	Connelly1	
Denmark	2 - 0	Bonetti	Cohen	Wilson	Stiles	Charlton J.1	Moore +	Ball	Greaves	Hurst G.	Eastham1	Connelly	
Poland	1 - 0	Banks G.	Cohen	Wilson	Stiles	Charlton J.	Moore +	Ball	Greaves	Charlton R.	Hunt1	Peters	
Uruguay	0 - 0	Banks G.	Cohen	Wilson	Stiles	Charlton J.	Moore +	Ball	Greaves	Charlton R.	Hunt	Connelly	
Mexico	2 - 0	Banks G.	Cohen	Wilson	Stiles	Charlton J.	Moore +	Paine	Greaves	Charlton R.1	Hunt1	Peters	
France	2 - 0	Banks G.	Cohen	Wilson	Stiles	Charlton J.	Moore +	Callaghan	Greaves	Charlton R.	Hunt2	Peters	
Argentina	1 - 0	Banks G.	Cohen	Wilson	Stiles	Charlton J.	Moore +	Ball	Hurst G.1	Charlton R.	Hunt	Peters	
Portugal	2 - 1	Banks G.	Cohen	Wilson	Stiles	Charlton J.	Moore +	Ball	Hurst G.	Charlton R.2	Hunt	Peters	
West Germany	4 - 2	Banks G.	Cohen	Wilson	Stiles	Charlton J.	Moore +	Ball	Hurst G.3	Charlton R.	Hunt	Peters1	

RESULTS AND TABLES

Two points for a win

GROUP ONE

	P	W	D	L	F	A	Pts
England (Q)	3	2	1	0	4	0	5
Uruguay (Q)	3	1	2	0	2	1	4
Mexico	3	0	2	1	1	3	2
France	3	0	1	2	1	5	1

11 July	England	0	Uruguay	0	Wembley
13 July	France	1	Mexico	1	Wembley
15 July	Uruguay	2	France	1	White City
16 July	England	2	Mexico	0	Wembley
	(R.Charlton, Hunt)				
19 July	Uruguay	0	Mexico	0	Wembley
20 July	England	2	France	0	Wembley
	(Hunt 2)				

GROUP TWO

	P	W	D	L	F	A	Pts
W. Germany (Q)	3	2	1	0	7	1	5
Argentina (Q)	3	2	1	0	4	1	5
Spain	3	1	0	2	4	5	2
Switzerland	3	0	0	3	1	9	0

12 July	W. Ger	5	Switz	0	Hillsborough
13 July	Argentina	2	Spain	1	Villa Park
15 July	Spain	2	Switz	1	Hillsborough
16 July	Argentina	0	W. Ger	0	Villa Park
19 July	Argentina	2	Switz	0	Hillsborough
20 July	W. Ger	2	Spain	1	Villa Park

GROUP FOUR

	P	W	D	L	F	A	Pts
USSR (Q)	3	3	0	0	6	1	6
N. Korea (Q)	3	1	1	1	2	4	3
Italy	3	1	0	2	2	2	2
Chile	3	0	1	2	2	5	1

12 July	USSR	3	N. Korea	0	Ayresome Park
13 July	Italy	2	Chile	0	Roker Park
15 July	Chile	1	N. Korea	1	Ayresome Park
16 July	USSR	1	Italy	0	Roker Park
19 July	N. Korea	1	Italy	0	Ayresome Park
20 July	USSR	2	Chile	1	Roker Park

GROUP THREE

	P	W	D	L	F	A	Pts
Portugal (Q)	3	3	0	0	9	2	6
Hungary (Q)	3	2	0	1	7	5	4
Brazil	3	1	0	2	4	6	2
Bulgaria	3	0	0	3	1	8	0

12 July	Brazil	2	Bulgaria	0	Goodison Park
13 July	Portugal	3	Hungary	1	Old Trafford
15 July	Hungary	3	Brazil	1	Goodison Park
16 July	Portugal	3	Bulgaria	0	Old Trafford
19 July	Portugal	3	Brazil	1	Goodison Park
20 July	Hungary	3	Bulgaria	1	Old Trafford

QUARTER-FINALS

23 July	England	1	Argentina	0	Wembley
	(Hurst)				
23 July	W. Ger	4	Uruguay	0	Hillsborough
23 July	Portugal	5	N. Korea	3	Goodison Park
23 July	USSR	2	Hungary	1	Roker Park

SEMI-FINALS

25 July	W. Ger	2	USSR	1	Goodison Park
26 July	England	2	Portugal	1	Wembley
	(R. Charlton 2)	(Eusébio (pen))			

THIRD PLACE PLAY-OFF

28 July	Portugal	2	USSR	1	Wembley

FINAL

30 July	England	4	W. Germany	2 (a.e.t.)	Wembley
	(Hurst 3, Peters)	(Haller, Weber)			

INDEX

Page numbers in *italics* indicate photographs.

ACKNOWLEDGEMENTS

The idea for this book in part evolved from a BBC TV documentary on England's victory in 1966, for which I acted as consultant. I am grateful to the producers for allowing access to the BBC's abundant and, in my view, underused, sporting archive. I would also like to thank Lorna Russell at Virgin Books for reviving the project in the first place, Lucy Oates, Simon Flavin of Mirrorpix, Pat Woods, Jane Morgan, and finally John Motson for writing the foreword and for his advice at all times.